You Can't Get Him Out of Your Mind . . .
So, what are you going to do about it?

☽

Seduce *any* man in the Zodiac
by discovering his astrological secrets.

●

*Cosmo*'s STAR SPELLS
will guide you from first glance to first date
to happily ever after.

☽

Learn:
* What drives *Aries* wild
* What the *Cancer* Man doesn't want you to know
* *Capricorn*'s idea of a perfect woman
* What you should never tell *Libra*
* *Scorpio*'s secret passion

○

and much more—
for each sign of the Zodiac.

*Other* **Cosmopolitan Books**

THE NICE GIRL'S GUIDE TO SENSATIONAL SEX
THE BEDSIDE ASTROLOGER COMPANION
IRMA KURTZ'S ULTIMATE PROBLEM SOLVER
WHAT MEN WANT FROM THE WOMEN THEY LOVE
ALL THE GOOD MEN ARE *NOT* TAKEN
IS HE THE RIGHT MAN FOR YOU?

*Look for These*
**Cosmopolitan Books**
*Coming Soon*

WHY DON'T YOU . . .
THE DATING GAME

# STAR SPELLS

### SARAH HOLCOMBE

**COSMOPOLITAN**

STAR SPELLS is an original publication of Cosmopolitan Books. This work has never before appeared in book form.

COSMOPOLITAN BOOKS
AVON BOOKS
A division of
The Hearst Corporation
1350 Avenue of the Americas
New York, New York 10019

Copyright © 1996 by Sarah Holcombe
Published by arrangement with the author
Library of Congress Catalog Card Number: 96-96040
ISBN: 0-380-77995-1

First Cosmopolitan Books Printing: August 1996

COSMOPOLITAN TRADEMARK REG. U.S. PAT. OFF. AND IN OTHER COUN-TRIES, MARCA REGISTRADA, HECHO EN U.S.A.

Printed in the U.S.A.

RA   10   9   8   7   6   5   4   3   2   1

# ACKNOWLEDGMENTS

I want to thank Nancy Kalish, my editor, for her unending generosity, wisdom, humor, and support from Day One, and for making this entire project a wonderful experience for me; Anda at the Bodhi Tree Bookstore in Los Angeles, for her clear-eyed explanations of the ascendant, or Rising Sign, and the importance of the Moon in relationships; and my husband, a magnificent example of Leo the Husband at his splendid best, who endured many take-out dinners, kept me inspired when inspiration was scarce, and has made of the song of my life a constant symphony.

# contents

| | |
|---|---|
| Introduction | 1 |
| His Moon | 3 |
| His Rising Sign | 5 |
| Aries | 8 |
| Taurus | 28 |
| Gemini | 49 |
| Cancer | 69 |
| Leo | 89 |
| Virgo | 109 |
| Libra | 130 |
| Scorpio | 150 |
| Sagittarius | 170 |
| Capricorn | 190 |
| Aquarius | 211 |
| Pisces | 229 |

○ (( ● )) )

# introduction

He's tall, he's dark, he's handsome—so now what? If you've always yearned for a step-by-step guide to the man of your dreams, yearn no more. Each chapter in this book is designed to maneuver you from first glance til death do you part (or til dawn do you part, whichever you prefer).

Before you begin, however, use the charts on the following pages to figure out your man's ascendant, or rising sign. This will help you construct the most comprehensive astrological portrait of him. Warning: rising signs can be deceptive! A brooding Scorpio with Aries rising is a suspiciously outgoing, friendly Scorpio. Don't be fooled. Read this book's chapter on his rising sign and get excellent clues to his worldly persona and outer personality.

And don't forget the Moon. A witty Gemini, with Mars in Aries, will come on like a dynamo, but he may fall apart in a crisis. Surprised? You won't be if you know his Moon is in Pisces. To learn more about how he will react to you emotionally, read his Moon sign as well. If you can't have his chart done, use the descriptive guide in "His Moon" on page 3 to learn more about this important part of his psyche.

Each chapter of this book begins at a party, where you can observe your man in his natural habitat. Designed like a comprehensive singles ad, the first three sections are written from the man's point of view so you can take a peek at what may be going on inside his head.

Next, see your Prince as he truly is, warts and all. Is your dashingly dominant Aries really a controlling cad? Learn how he fools himself and what kind of numbers he'll try to run on you and why. Look through his private pair of rose-colored glasses as he stares at the woman of his dreams—how she walks, smiles, and tosses her hair. You'll find that this information can be quite useful when you turn to the section "His Sexual Secrets and Desires."

However, you'll find that whether it's power, control, or freedom, all men like something better than sex. Find out what it is in "Afterglow: What You Need to Know"; you'll understand the difference between what he wants and what he needs from you, and how to give him both. And be sure to read "Make It Forever," which tells you what you need in order to make your relationship last a lifetime—whether it's your own mutual fund, a flourishing career, or detente with his mother.

To know all is to love all. His smiles, his frowns, his moods and his dreams aren't really any stranger than yours, after all. May *Star Spells* guide you to a deeper understanding of your prince, and may you have more fun, sex, and romance together than you ever dreamed possible.

○ (( ● )) ☽

# his moon

In addition to your man's rising sign, it's important to know what his Moon is. While your man's social, civilized side is apparent in his rising sign, his Moon governs his emotional life, and thus many of his emotional reactions to you. To locate his Moon, find out his birthday (the time is not necessary) and then go to your local bookshop and look up his Moon in an ephemeris, the astrological guide.

No time for research? To make an educated guess, observe your man's emotional reactions and match them to the Moon listed below that seems the closest.

Here are some general characteristics for each Moon:

**ARIES MOON:** Direct. Aggressive. Impulsive. Perhaps volatile. Emotionally honest. Sudden tempers are soon forgotten.

**TAURUS MOON:** A need for financial security in order to feel safe. Beauty- and nature-loving. Materialistic. Lazy. Calm.

**GEMINI MOON:** Fickle. Fresh. Frivolous. Flippant. Talkative. Superficial. Vacillating. Could end up with several marriages.

**CANCER MOON:** Withdrawn. Indirect. Touchy. Oversensitive. Intense. Possibly psychic. Home-loving. Emotionally smothering. Security-loving.

**LEO MOON:** Dramatic. Very romantic. Affectionate. Wants to look good. Wants beloved and family to look good. Generous. Domineering.

**VIRGO MOON:** Practical. Hardworking. Neat. Perfectionistic. Interested in health to promote emotional well-being.

**LIBRA MOON:** Charming. Elegant. Emotionally dependent. Seeks balance. People-loving. Good at public relations.

**SCORPIO MOON:** Extremely intense. Strong-willed. Possessive. Brooding. Very loyal. Obssesive. Takes things personally.

**SAGITTARIUS MOON:** Idealistic. Unrealistic. Lover of travel and social issues. Gets hung up occasionally on philosophical beliefs.

**CAPRICORN MOON:** Reserved. Cautious. Ambitious. Responsible. Calculating. Seeks financial security. Depressive.

**AQUARIUS MOON:** Humanitarian. Stubborn. Seeks personal and universal freedom of expression. Shy about emotional involvement. Maddenly remote.

**PISCES MOON:** Mind reader. Coy. Touchy. Sensitive. Neurotic. Vulnerable. Highly imaginative. Artistic. Sympathetic. Easily hurt.

○ ( ( ● ) ) )

# his rising sign

The powerful rising sign is the social personality of the individual—which means it's usually highly conscious and developed. It's the mask your man wears in public, and it can fool you. However, if you know what his rising sign is, you can be prepared and use it—along with the information in the chapter on his particular sign—to know and understand the *real* him.

To find your man's rising sign, ask him what time he was born. The sun rises in the rising sign from 4:00–6:00 A.M. at the time of birth, and the sign changes every two hours after that. For example, an Aries born at 5:00 A.M. would have an Aries rising sign. An Aries born at 12:00 noon would have Leo rising. See chart below. Was he born at noon? For men born on the cusp, read both rising signs and see which one fits. For complete accuracy, consult an ephemeris or have your man's chart done by a professional.

|               | Aries | Taurus | Gemini | Cancer | Leo |
|---------------|-------|--------|--------|--------|-----|
| 4:00–6:00 A.M. | Ari | Tau | Gem | Can | Leo |
| 6:00–8:00 A.M. | Tau | Gem | Can | Leo | Vir |
| 8:00–10:00 A.M. | Gem | Can | Leo | Vir | Lib |
| 10:00 A.M.–12:00 NOON | Can | Leo | Vir | Lib | Sco |
| 12:00 NOON–2:00 P.M. | Leo | Vir | Lib | Sco | Sag |
| 2:00–4:00 P.M. | Vir | Lib | Sco | Sag | Cap |
| 4:00–6:00 P.M. | Lib | Sco | Sag | Cap | Aqu |
| 6:00–8:00 P.M. | Sco | Sag | Cap | Aqu | Pis |
| 8:00–10:00 P.M. | Sag | Cap | Aqu | Pis | Ari |
| 10:00–12:00 P.M. | Cap | Aqu | Pis | Ari | Tau |
| 12:00 P.M.–2:00 A.M. | Aqu | Pis | Ari | Tau | Gem |
| 2:00–4:00 A.M. | Pis | Ari | Tau | Gem | Can |

| Virgo | Libra | Scorpio | Sagittarius | Capricorn | Aquarius | Pisces |
|-------|-------|---------|-------------|-----------|----------|--------|
| Vir | Lib | Sco | Sag | Cap | Aqu | Pis |
| Lib | Sco | Sag | Cap | Aqu | Pis | Ari |
| Sco | Sag | Cap | Aqu | Pis | Ari | Tau |
| Sag | Cap | Aqu | Pis | Ari | Tau | Gem |
| Cap | Aqu | Pis | Ari | Tau | Gem | Can |
| Aqu | Pis | Ari | Tau | Gem | Can | Leo |
| Pis | Ari | Tau | Gem | Can | Leo | Vir |
| Ari | Tau | Gem | Can | Leo | Vir | Lib |
| Tau | Gem | Can | Leo | Vir | Lib | Sco |
| Gem | Can | Leo | Vir | Lib | Sco | Sag |
| Can | Leo | Vir | Lib | Sco | Sag | Cap |
| Leo | Vir | Lib | Sco | Sag | Cap | Aqu |

# aries

## MARCH 21 - APRIL 20

### BEST LOVE MATCHES

Aries & Gemini
Aries & Leo
Aries & Sagittarius
Aries & Aquarius

He's reckless, dashing, and he's using up all the available oxygen in the room. He talks fast. He moves fast. He's got courage to die for. He's looking for the ultimate dare. He's Aries, the Ram.

### FAMOUS ARIENS

Marlon Brando, Alec Baldwin, David Letterman, Danny DeVito, Paul Reiser, Colin Powell, James Woods, Robert Downey, Jr., Andy Garcia, Gary Oldman, Matthew Modine

## I AM

Positively insane about you. Who are you? Why
have you been ignoring me for the last fifty-five
minutes of this party? So what if I've only just arrived. I knew something magical was about to happen. You have spectacular eyes. Ignore all those
people I so rudely interrupted to come over here.
They need a little excitement in their lives. Besides,
being ignored by me is kind of a compliment.

Normally I don't notice anyone anyway—active
ignoring takes energy. Speaking of energy, look at
me! I'm a few quarts low. I haven't been to bed in
the last thirty-six hours—the killer whales are here.
Every time killer whales are spotted along the
coast, I beep everybody and we drop everything
and race down and jump in with them. I'm the
leader. Last night I swam five miles—you should
see what whales look like by moonlight. Like wet
angels drenched in dark silk; when I touch them I
feel as if I'm making love to the sea itself. . . . Of
course, last night it rained. But that was fun because the fog rolled in and we couldn't tell if they
were whales or sharks. I've gotten to know this one
whale like my brother.

Afraid? I've never been afraid of anything in my
life. Want to hear about the time I faced down a
grizzly? Yeah, that's the scar. I don't tell just anyone about these things, you know—super athletes
should be humble, don't you think? Besides, I'm
kind of shy.

This party is much too mellow—mellow people
get on my nerves. How can human beings just
stand around like this? Don't they have lives? I
should set off these firecrackers I brought with me.
I was going to wait for midnight, but what the hell.

I know! Let's tango! Go tell those guys to play
something Latin—I'll get everybody rounded up.
They'll thank me for this. You don't tango? You do
now. And you're spending the rest of the evening
with me. Don't argue. You'll never win.

My God, you're beautiful. You look like a Mo-
digliani come to life. A thousand women would kill
to look like you. What? Of course that's recidivist
and chauvinistic! The world needs more recidivist
and chauvinistic gratitude for women's beauty!
You agree? Disagree? What?! Don't quit on me, for
God's sake! You're not swallowing my opinions
wholesale, are you? I certainly hope not! I'd be
bored to death! And it's a colossal mistake to bore
me, gorgeous. . . .

No, you don't want to make any mistakes with
me just yet. You're interested. I can tell by the
cover-girl sneer. You think this arrogant, bump-
tious little-boy act is all there is, don't you? You
think you're better than that. You think I'm a
clumsy little stud-puppy, and you'd eat me alive,
would you? I wouldn't want to burst your assump-
tions, so I'll just mosey over there and see if that
blonde wants any help with her chip and dip. . . .
Oh, you don't want me to go just yet? Yeah, you're
interested. You're more than interested. Don't let
go of the sneer; it works. Look at me. I like that. I
know what your opinion of me is—I can see it in
your eyes. And it doesn't bother me a bit.

I promised we'd row across the lake tonight and
check out this private cabin of a friend of mine.
They've had some prowlers lately. It's a secluded
little place in the middle of the woods. There's a
genuine Franklin stove and a bottle of Krug in the
fridge. How do I know? I placed it there before I came
to the party. I knew it was a night for magic. . . .

Your arms look strong. You row, don't you? Good! I'll navigate by starlight—just like Columbus. I knew you'd come. I always get what I want. You're mesmerizing me and I'm having the same effect on you—admit it! And you're coming with me tonight if I have to carry you there myself.

## YOU ARE

One drop-dead dame. You make every milliliter of my blood explode. You have an aura of power even without me. You are the ultimate dare. A nod from you is like a summons to the contest of my life.

One thing I adore about you is that you fight back. I'm so bossy I don't see how I stand myself. I prefer the word commanding, but the plain truth is, I'm bossy. That's because I know how to do everything better than anyone else. But enough about me.

When we argue, you aren't thrown by a few minor temper tantrums—you throw them right back. I love a good fight! It makes the sex so much more spectacular! Furthermore, I can't walk all over you. This shocks and thrills me, since I use most people as throwaway rugs. Don't repeat that, but it's true.

You make innocence unspeakably erotic. Your sexual tastes are as wide-ranging as mine, and yet you seem magically, maddeningly untouched by it all. I don't want to make love—that is for lesser mortals. I want to explode into a thousand tiny stars and leave the Earth behind. I want to see God in the dark face of night. You alone know how to take me there.

Your have a sense of adventure—more than that—you can visit Jupiter without leaving your chair. But we do leave, frequently, because I intend

to see every country in the world before I die, and
you're coming with me. And your forty pieces of
matched luggage don't faze me. I'll just leave them
on the tarmac once we hit Tibet.

You separate the men from the boys. Then you
walk all over the boys, in those $600 bad-girl
pumps from Manolo Blanik, until you could drop
from boredom. Secretly you long to be dominated,
but no one's ever been able to tell you to siddown
and shaddup, and lived to tell the tale. Put on some
more of that No. 5 Red lipstick, baby, and sit back.
Your luck is about to change.

## HOW TO DRIVE ME WILD

First of all, I want to watch how you play me. I
want you to see you play me like a violin, there,
from across the room. I want throngs of men
around you, while you stand there in your chic little nothing and those mile-high shoes. Send me signals with your body. Me alone. When I catch your
eye, saunter off to the balcony. Ignore me just
enough to let me know you don't come cheap. In
fact, you don't come at all. For anyone. Except me.
When we finally speak, keep it up. I've heard
you're witty. Prove it. Challenge me. Give me that
seductive indifference that drives me insane. Keep
it up until I have to stop your mouth with a kiss
that will last until dawn, far away from here.

When we're alone, you can drop your shtick
along with those three ounces of silk you're wearing. I don't want to touch you at first. Not yet. I
simply want to watch you, by firelight. I want you
to take down your hair and walk for me; I want to
see your bare feet on some old hardwood floor.
Don't. Talk. I hate sophistication in bed. I want it

to be the first time, every time. I don't want your body; I want your soul. Surprised? Didn't think a gloryhound like me would want to drink you in like communion wine? Shut up. Don't. Talk.

Now sit down. On my lap, where else? You look like a dancer. Turn up that music. I want to watch you to lap-dance, now, on me. I want you to see how you make me hard. That's it. Pretend I'm your best customer. See if you can make me come. Caress me. You've never done this before? You're superb. Don't stop. Don't talk. Don't stop.

## CONFIDENTIALLY YOURS

### ✻ What He Won't Tell You

So many women, so little time . . . sigh. . . . He's not addicted to you. He's addicted to his own adrenaline. Never forget this. When his passion is inflamed by your eager response, he's getting his nightly fix. Think of him as a friendly vampire who needs every last drop of excitement you can provide in order to live and love another day.

If he loved you tonight, will he know you tomorrow? The fruit fly lives for a day and a half. Think of all the love, sex and death it has to cram into thirty-six hours. And if you had to bet on whether your basic Ram or your basic fruit fly has a longer attention span, bet on the fly.

He thinks super-athletes ought to be humble. That's nice. In Ram-speak, the word "humble" means that he tells you he's magnificent, personally, before anyone else can botch the job. And *shy*? Well, he's terribly insecure. Aries experiences emotional insecurity as shyness. It's not.

The Ram is an intensely sexual creature. There

are nights when anything on two legs makes him ravenous. The sexual act to Aries is an explosion of primitive drives—erotic, sensual, sexual, romantic, spiritual, intellectual, emotional, as well as hunger, thirst, the life force . . . even Thanatos, the death instinct, is in there somewhere. You may never sleep again, you may be sore in interesting places, but if his passion is genuinely aroused, he will make sure you never, ever forget him.

All Aries have a way of squeezing time until one hour becomes two. He thinks fast, he acts fast, he even breathes faster than you do. Thus, he is never on time for a date. He's supposed to pick you up at 7:30 and it's only 7:15? Hey! He's got fifteen minutes! Why not wax the car before he goes? This behavior will *never* change, so if you're a stickler for punctuality, flee now or bring a good book to all your rendezvous.

Notice how often war terms come up with Aries. He doesn't just understand you, he wrestles to understand you. He fights his way to your side, and his jokes will slay you (they had better), as he battles to make himself understood. Aries is ruled by Mars, god of war, and he is never fully alive unless he is fighting tooth and nail. So if you've always yearned for life on the edge, by all means hang on as he gallops off toward a distant windmill. Remember, a battle a day keeps the doctor away.

## * The Bad Stuff

Is he self-absorbed? Can you spell Narcissus? He was the guy who spent his life gazing at himself in a pool. Eventually he angered Aphrodite, goddess of love, who explained to this moron that he was wasting his time on the wrong love object. Narcissus didn't agree, so she turned him into a plant. Think about it.

Most people glance at themselves occasionally as they pass a mirror. Aries, however, never passes up this chance to sooth his anxieties. What if he looked in the mirror and he had (gasp!) aged? This is the sun sign of personal vanity, so don't be shocked if he gives you a his-and-hers lipo job for Christmas.

He doesn't really set the world record for speed sex, silly. Rabbits do. And no, his idea of foreplay isn't literally ripping your clothes off—with repeated instruction, you can actually train him to use the zipper. And sex with him isn't exactly Slam, Bam, Thank You Ma'am. That's Slam *Dunk* to you, baby, and best you appreciate your lucky day! Not everyone has the privilege of sleeping with an Aries male. He hasn't made it to Bulgaria yet, and there's half of Australia to go.

When the Ram falls in love, when he's completely devastated by you—robbed of speech, even—he's achieved one of his favorite conditions in life. He expends an incredible amount of energy just to get to that dizzying, head-over-teacup point of no return. Any attractive woman will do. So write your name on your forehead before making love, like a homemade cue card. That way he'll feel free to address you personally when his Moment of Truth arrives. And it gives the whole muscular rendezvous a nice intimate touch.

Does he call when he's supposed to? Does he show up on time? Chuckle, chuckle. This is The One Your Mother Warned You About. Of course, he shows up on time—Ram time. Of course, he calls when he is supposed to—when he calls, that's when he's supposed to.

He doesn't have much of a temper. No. And Vlad

the Impaler was kind to his dachsunds. If you're an Aries or a Leo, you may be able to withstand the nuclear holocaust of his displeasure. If you're any other sign, hide under the bed. Get yourself a soundproof closet with a triple police lock. And make him promise something exceptional before you unbar the door.

### ✳ How Aries Likes His Women

The Ram prefers to be excited past the point of delirium, just to be sure he's really in love. Rescuing your gerbil from the jaws of the local pit bull, climbing through your bedroom window when you've barred him from the house in a pitiful attempt to get some sleep, nuclear lovemaking that destroys every stick of furniture on the second floor—this! This is romance!

Therefore, you don't make it easy—in fact, you make it just this side of impossible. No man can win you, except just possibly the Ram, and you make him sweat for it until he's so aroused he's barely in control. You make him prove his value—something he loves to do—and yet you believe in him completely.

Furthermore, you are smart, assertive, and extremely independent. You have a powerful personality. You have so many sides to you that it would take a lifetime to encounter them all. So, have a life. No, have an interesting life. No, have a romance novel you're living out, in full technicolor glory, that you casually invite him to share. If he has the guts.

### ✳ What The Ram Sees When He Looks At You

The Ram is ruled by Mars, God of War, which makes you no less than Venus, Goddess of Love, his only possible consort. This is just about the size of his ego projection, too, so it's only fair to warn you. You are gorgeous, powerful, and with a string of achievements. You know your worth. You insist on being amused, wined, dined, entertained, and challenged. Can you keep up with him? What an amusing question. Can he keep up with you? Your combination of virtues will fry every neuron he has into molten ectoplasm.

## ✳ What Turns Him On

Excitement. Drama. The thrill of the chase. The unexpected hint, suggestion, cue; the surprise meeting; the clandestine look; the seismic tremor of a sidelong glance. God, does this man love drama! He wants—no, he demands—to be enchanted. He seeks She Who Casts No Ordinary Spell. The problem is, he'll go through several thousand ladies-in-waiting just to find her. This isn't promiscuity, though; this is his personal and very thorough search for Her.

## ✳ What Rules The Ram

His need to be first. This is not an adult need, but the charming urge of a three-year-old to be the first one in the ocean on a hot June day. He really does have more energy than you, your baby Rottweiler, and an entire soccer team. So he really *can* race you to the water and win every single time, see? Winning, to Aries, is just psychic energy conservation. No use holding him back; he might implode.

# THE CHASE

## ✳ His Secret Paradox

He needs your unwavering loyalty and undying support, but he needs you to keep him just the teensiest bit off balance. Got that? So have absolute faith in his talent, give him thunderous applause for all his victories, and let him know that although you love him with all your heart, you do need to be stimulated, challenged, aroused and inspired, and what has he done for you lately?

P.S.—This social charmer is a secret loner who can, and in fact prefers to, fend for himself for long periods of time. Notice how few close friends he actually has. He likes people, but he doesn't need them as much as it appears. Don't be fooled by the swarms of admirers. They're just window dressing.

## ✳ How To Bewitch Aries

Dare him. There is not an Arien corpuscle that can resist a dare. Have him save you from something dangerous. In their daydreams, all Rams charge around on a snowy steed, mashing enemies to dust. Aries is a magnificent warrior, so let him fight for you, while you watch in starstruck awe as he sends foe after foe screaming into oblivion.

Then there is an attitude you have, a way of discussing politics, or sushi, that is undeniably erotic. You ignore the effect you're having on him. It doesn't exist. You don't mention a word of sex; you don't broach anything remotely near it. You talk, and you laugh, and you completely ignore the growing tension you see in him, as he wonders if he's getting to you, or if he's gone completely crazy. You give nothing away. What's to give away? You merely wanted his opinion on man's capacity for moral purity; it's been haunting you lately. *He* hasn't been haunting you, heavens no! When he tells you you are incredibly beautiful, you act as if he'd reported the weather. You thank him politely. You keep this up all evening, all week, and the week after that. When he begins to look thin and haunted, you are kindness itself. . . . When he gets that lost, starving look in his eyes, mention that you've never had one perfect kiss.

## \* Don't . . .

Use the word w-e-a-k when you're within shouting distance. Ignore him. Ignore him while you're sleeping. Ignore him when you're all alone, eating tomato soup on a rainy day—he has state-of-the-art attention radar. Toddle off with your vibrator and tell him you'll catch him later. Keep secrets. Flirt with other men, if you value your life. Think of flirting with other men. Look the plumber in the eye as he bends down to fix the toilet. Tell your Ram you don't believe in miracles.

## \* Who He Likes To Bed

His current love, his ex-love, his future fantasy, the redhead who glanced at him on the train this morning, the blonde who returned his stare over her newspaper, the waitress who served him his chocolate doughnut, the new receptionist at work, the bay of secretaries to his right, the bay of secretaries to his left, his favorite client, his favorite client's sister, mother, mother-in-law, aunt, best friend, college roommate . . . and it's only 8:00 A.M.! He can keep this up until he breaks for sleep sometime around midnight. Make sure you are the ultimate challenge, which he can't resist. And be glad he's only interested in *half* the human race.

## ✱ Who He Likes To Wed

Someone deeply kind. Someone who sticks by him through every crazed adventure he can dream up. He can be fabulously loyal and superbly tender when he finally relinquishes his heart (note the verb), and he will outdo himself to surpass your expectations. So expect the moon. Aries is a born superachiever, but he desperately needs someone to carry his spiritual torch. Give him all your faith, never doubt him for an instant, encircle him in infinite kindness, and he will prove a dazzling, endearing, and absolutely steadfast mate. Just wait til he grows up *before* you do all this.

## ✱ What He's Secretly Afraid Of

Possibly you don't like him. Winning isn't everything. There is no Easter Bunny. His shyness is not shyness, just instability. Subtle people have the advantage over him; he doesn't know why. God is in the details. Women would rather have sex with modest, patient men. All the really exciting stuff happened before he was born. It's a kinder, gentler era. If he falls asleep, he'll miss something. He could grow up if he really wanted to.

## ✱ When To Say Yes

Say yes when you are overwhelmed, when you are beyond words, when you are warm, soft clay in his godlike hands. Don't bother saying yes before this, because the Arien ego demands that you be brought to this point. Anything less is for peasants.

# THE COUP DE GRACE

## ✻ His Sexual Secrets And Desires

He has the energy of the solar system, the stamina of the Marines, and the brain of Winnie the Pooh when it comes to romance. He wants you completely available to him, but don't make it easy. He wants you sophisticated enough to drive him crazy, yet innocence itself in the boudoir. Furthermore, he is the ultimate performer, out to give you a religious experience.

The moment has arrived, heralded by champagne and moonlight. He picks you up and carries you all the way to bed. He remembered you told him how you longed to be carried. You can't believe his strength. You hold out your arms to be undressed, slowly; you are embarrassed. He is stupefied by your shyness, and it touches a place in him he has never known.

Silently, you stand there as the clothes fall from your body. You can barely look at him as he stares at your body standing perfectly still in the moonlight. You have never done this before. Well, not like this. You allow him to lead you to the bed. You make it clear that you need protection, that you are unsure, that all your verbal sophistication was a mask for the innocence within. Your bashful awkwardness is rendering him senseless with desire. You unpin your hair. You have never let your hair down in front of him. So many firsts tonight.

You bend to kiss him, taking his head in your hands, kissing his eyelids, the delicate hair on his face, the soft area above and around his mouth. Tell me a secret, you say, laughing, and you keep kissing him until he does. You won't let him kiss you.

Tell me another, you laugh as you lower your face to his chest and begin to lick his nipples until they stiffen. You demand to hear a secret, and another, and another, until you have reached his penis, which you massage with your hair, as you lower your mouth to the soft, secret underside of his balls, which you also massage, softly with your hair. You lick his balls until he begins to moan softly; then you stop. You circle his penis with your face, again and again, slower and slower, and you reach for him with the tip of your tongue. You are reminded of your favorite ice cream cone; you cannot get enough of him. You raise your face so he can watch as you slide your tongue up and then down, up and down, licking him like an animal who has been starved for food. This food. When you find yourself sitting on top of him, riding him, you don't know how it happened.

Tell me what to do, you whisper as you stare at him. You are terrified by your own lust. You need someone to obey. He is the most masterful man you've ever known. As he begins to tell you his desires, you ride him like a huge, dark wave, sliding up and down—and you feel it happening. Something inside changes and you become an animal, something you are not familiar with. You begin to make noises that you have not heard before, back in your throat. You don't take your eyes off him as he stares at you and tells you that he wants you to come. You begin to tremble so hard that you are in danger of blacking out as you ride him into outer space and every cell in your body explodes like a new star.

You have never behaved like this before, you whisper as you lie there, unable to move. What has he done to you? Sleeping with him is like sleeping with a god. He has taken you to that country where each of you enters a state of blind heat that is almost holy, it is so pure. . . . Would he, could he do this again? Now?

## * Shhh . . .

Make sure he finds you making breakfast in the nude at least once a month—a breakfast of edible flowers, a glass of Roderer, and *you*.

# AFTERGLOW: WHAT YOU NEED TO KNOW

### * What Aries Likes Better Than Sex

Winning. If he can't win at least twice a day, he turns into one miserable sheep.

### * Will He Marry His Best Lover Or Best Friend?

He will marry the only girl of his once and future dreams, she whom the stars picked out for him centuries ago, and there will be angel trumpets and flowers from paradise raining on his nuptials. In heaven, Shakespeare will write a new sonnet at the moment of his first marital climax, and Cupid will personally hover over his marital bed. He actually believes this, so study it. It can be useful.

### * What He Wants From You

Admiration, challenge, admiration, wonder, awe, and admiration. Aries and Aquarius are both performers, but unlike Aquarius, with the Ram you always know where you stand. Front row center, and turn up the applause, thank you. Admiring him is like filling his gas tank—it keeps him run-

ning smoothly for another 100 miles. So praise him,
congratulate him, and make it verbal, verbal, verbal. If your faucet of praise has developed a leak,
he will be aghast. What is wrong? Did you fail to
perceive his charm this morning?

## ✷ What He Needs From You

The peripatetic, powerful, combative Ram needs
your faith. He needs you to believe that hidden beneath (way beneath) his fickle, wild facade there
beats a true and tender heart. And behind that restless, jack-of-all-trades daredevil is a powerful master of the arts or business, who will make his mark
upon an astonished world. If you give this man
your undying, unwavering loyalty and support,
you will produce *wonders* together.

## ✷ What He Won't Give Up For You

Winning. Conquering. Getting what he wants when
he wants it. The Ram's metabolism is actually low-
ered in situations of frustration and stagnation. Besides, should you be his Chosen One, it is his great
joy to lay his trophies at your feet. Try to guide his
conquering urge *outward*, toward the world at
large. White-water rafting, helicopter skiing, the
Cup races, the Indy 500—these are safe and ap-
proved outlets for the Arian need to triumph at all
costs.

## ✷ What He Will Give Up For You

You've read *Hero of a Thousand Faces*? Well, pretend
the faces are all female and you've got the key to
the ultimate Aries fantasy. Believe it or not, however, the Ram will settle down and devote himself

to the woman he deems his eternal mate. His eternal mate, however, had better be worth this once-in-a-lifetime change of persona. That's why he takes so long to find her.

## ✳ How To Make Him Fall In Love With You, Really

You've heard of the Child Within? Focus on the Ewe Within. The Ram needs tenderness—unbelievable, unspeakable tenderness. The vulnerability of this man is awesome, although you'd never know it, since he is the master of the zodiac at concealing emotional pain. Aries inspired the phrase "The best defense is a good offense." Show him that you honor his virtues, which are courage, honesty, and loyalty, and that you expect him to live up to them always. The Ram has been waiting all his life for someone to demand that he live up to his better self. Once he figures out that you carry his soul engraved on your heart, Lancelot will be yesterday's news compared to your indomitable Ram. So ask him to be your knight in shining armor. Ask with your whole heart and soul, and he will never, ever let you down.

## ✳ Make It Forever

The Ram is secretly looking for someone to come home to. But the thought of home bores and disturbs Aries. He's heard of domestic bliss, yes, but to him it sounds like a skin disease. Show him that home with the right companion—witty, funny, adventurous, casual, sexy, skilled and *independent*—can be the ultimate adventure. His astonishment and gratitude will last the rest of his life.

P.S.—If the Ram is late again, has forgotten to call, or was only asking that blond model for directions, make it *very* clear that charming apologies don't make it the tenth time around. He will confess his errant ways so innocently, with such sincere sorrow, that you will think you have stumbled upon the ideal man. Until tomorrow, when he does it again, and confesses so innocently and so sincerely that you could brain him with your Cuisinart.

## CRUCIAL MINUTIAE

### ✳ What To Feed Aries

Just call him Old Iron Innards—he can choke down absolutely anything, and does. One Aries we know lived for years on french fries, doughnuts, and beer. Upon examination, he was found to be in flawless health. The doctor asked him what he did to achieve such perfection. "Guinness and grease," the Ram replied modestly.

But help your Ram do battle against his worst tendencies (put it that way—it'll work). Feed him mellow meals filled with comforting carbohydrates like rice, root vegetables, and home-baked bread. Introduce him to fruits and decaffeinated teas. Once he discovers the soothing relationship of food and peace, he may allow you to calm him down like this more often.

### ✳ How To Take Care Of Your Ram

The Aries metabolism is the eighth wonder of the world—the Ram has rude, crude, and terribly attractive health, twenty-four hours a day. But Rams are careless of their energy. So suggest that it might be fun to go to bed before 2 A.M. and actually sleep—who knows what adventure lurks in his dreams? And heaven knows, he really doesn't need three cups of espresso—either you or his gallbladder will give out from the strain. If he won't exercise, no problem. Take him to a karate exhibition. He'll have signed up before you leave.

## ✳ For His Birthday

Giving presents to a Ram is extremely gratifying—it's like watching a Christmas tree light up all by itself. And this is one sign that will spoil you in return, no matter what his current income level. The Ram will somehow hint that he's a thinker, or an intellectual, so give him a book with fascinating theories, or tickets to a great lecture or new play. He'll enjoy testing himself against the mental hardware of famous public figures. Succor his vanity with the perfect cashmere sweater or a fabulous leather bomber jacket. But to really thrill him, give him an adventure! Try a scuba course, ski trip, parachute lessons, or a trip to King Arthur's original court, where he can groove on Lancelot, the ultimate Aries. Out of ideas? Embroider the words *C'est Moi*, on his pajamas.

○《●》》

*Christian 5-11-67*
*Kyle*

# taurus

## APRIL 21 · MAY 21

### BEST LOVE MATCHES

Taurus & Cancer
Taurus & Virgo
Taurus & Capricorn
Taurus & Pisces

At the party, he's the one standing quietly by the punch bowl, where he can satisfy his appetite and survey the goings-on with his customary composure. He's quietly imposing and can be very funny. He's also unruffled, amused, and in control. He's Taurus, the Bull.

## FAMOUS TAUREANS

William Shakespeare, Al Pacino, George Clooney, Jay Leno, Jean Paul Gaultier, Jack Nicholson, Billy Joel, Christian LaCroix, Daniel Day-Lewis, Jerry Seinfeld, Pierce Brosnan, David Keith

## I AM

Calm. So calm. It's contentment itself over here by the punch bowl and the cookies. These crazy people are extremely amusing; imagine wasting all that energy. They must have so much to prove. Tsk. I have nothing to prove. To anyone. If I stand here, eventually everyone will have to come over for refreshment. Then I can talk to them or not. I believe in economy of energy. I hate waste with a passion; thus, I never waste. That's why I'll retire in my early fifties and grow roses. Oh yes, I've been planning my retirement since I was seven. It may take me a while, but I always get where I'm going.

I don't mind being compared to Ferdinand, the Bull with the Delicate Ego. Although nothing about me is delicate. Except the feeling in my fingers when I touch you. Touching is music. Talk is not; frankly, most people can put a lid on it, for my money. But Ferdinand—now Ferdinand would rather sit in a pasture all day, sniffing daisies, than go face some imbecile matador. He was one smart stud. Me, I can spend hours contemplating the color of an orchid.

These cookies are god-awful. I'm only eating them to see if they get any better. You should try mine sometime. I spent last Saturday experimenting with chocolate filo dough, all alone in the kitchen. Don't deny it. You assume someone who wears tailored grey flannel can't cook, but you're wrong. The kitchen is my second-favorite room in life. The home, after all, is the most important place on earth. You get your well-lit kitchen with lots of work space, you get your decent-sized bedroom with your custom-built bed, flannel sheets, thick pile carpet, maybe a little refrigerator hidden away in the night table, God! Who would leave? I never do.

I hate people who hate routine. Without routine, morals would collapse. Look at this party. I've been coming here for years, and now they introduce these New Age bean sprout cookies and some kind of seltzer music! Seltzer, salsa, what's the difference? What was wrong with chocolate chip and Benny Goodman? And look at this table here! Is this a table or a tree? Can't they decide? What is so difficult about leaving things the way they are?? Look at the result! Collapse!! Today, a tree; tomorrow, the government!

Furthermore, I am not a young fogey, contrary to popular rumor. Young fogeys do not linger for hours over a bottle of good burgundy—several bottles, as a matter of fact. Young fogeys do not dream of lying naked on a private sand dune, well protected from the wind and sand, applying edible suntan oil to every part of your body. Do young fogeys know how to marinate a decent lamb? I thought not.

I've been noticing you all evening, but I haven't come over to say hello yet. I'll stand here, telling jokes, cracking up the guests, secretly watching you. I'm not shy, God forbid. I simply do not go for this Full Disclosure Act that most people feel is necessary on a first date. Don't tell me! Tell your psychiatrist! That was a joke. You hardly look like you need a psychiatrist. Me either.

I am strong—so strong I may frighten you at first. You have never seen a will this powerful. When my desires get past the slow-boil stage, when I have decided you are mine, there will be no place you can hide. But don't be afraid. I am gentle, and tenderness itself with my beloved. I may be plain-spoken, but I carry poetry in my fingertips—just how much will stun you when we are naked together. I am all of those old-fashioned things that never go out of style: dependable, loyal, nurturing, and deeply loving. When I find you, I'm strictly a one-woman man.

## YOU ARE

Real. That's what I love most about you. You have a beautiful, generous body; when I hold you, there is something to squeeze. You are not one of those atmospheric creatures, all air and bones, who lives on broccoli and chocolate. You have hips, and thighs, and breasts like hills in southern Spain. When I see you naked, I forget who I am: I could spend hours fingering each strand of your hair. And I will, oh, I will.

I love how honest you are. I can't stand those female guessing games; I never get the point. Furthermore, your sensuality matches mine. You could spend an entire weekend commuting between the jacuzzi and the bed, with pit stops at the margarita pitcher.

You are as skilled and efficient at your career as you are in the kitchen, and I admire the way you take care of yourself financially. Yet you are not power-hungry. There is no "first place" in our bed; rather, we sleep in the spoon position, side by side. Well, with me on the outside, to protect you in case of burglars or storms.

And you simply adore being female. You feel no need to politically defend your love of home, your cooking skills, or the way you sewed the draperies for your breakfast nook. Or, last but not least, your need to shower me with neck massages, homemade muffins, chicken soup, and babies. Babies? Of course! I'm a natural Daddy! I wants lots of little "you's" and "me's" running around—the more, the merrier. You are my dear love, but you are more—you give my life its meaning.

## HOW TO DRIVE ME WILD

I don't need words. I never have. It has taken me time to want you this much, but that's fine. Desire should simmer, just under boil, for a long, lazy time. So now we know each other a little. I like how you don't flirt with everyone in the room; I like it that you're a little quiet, and private.

Now. It's a lazy Friday afternoon. Lock the front door and unplug the phone. I don't think we'll emerge til sometime on Sunday, do you? I thought not. You're very beautiful right now. I love your bedroom; it looks like a den hidden deep in the forest. I love that feeling. No, don't try and take off my clothes. I'll tell you when. Some have called me plodding. I call it deliberate. Lie back on those silk sheets—nice choice, by the way—and be still. Let me slip off one of your shoes. Just your shoe, for now. Why are you impatient? I intend to inhale you, inch by beautiful, naked inch, and I'll start with your feet.

Don't ever think you can push me. I want to savor you. Savoring takes time. I want to meditate on your slender, delicate foot; I want to inhale your scent and taste it on my tongue. By the way, I like these scented pillows. And I appreciate the wine you've poured—how many bottles do you have? A case? Good.

After your feet, I will undress the rest of you and

lay you back on these pale, woven pillows. I will rub your body with almond oil until it gleams in the candlelight, until the sight of you is the only light in the room. If I unroll these chocolate leaves, will you feed them to me, one at a time, on your tongue? When you are covered with oil, come sit on me. Let me get supremely comfortable. Open another bottle. These silk sheets feel like warm water on my skin. Just sit on my chest. Let me stare at you, while I sip. I'm not ready, just yet. I want to watch you past your embarrassment, past your shyness, until I can see the desire grow in your face; until you want me to do it, you want to move up and you want me to enter you slowly, with my tongue; until you want to watch me drink until the tremors start all over you and you begin to move in circles from desire.

Don't try to take over. I don't like that. When I've watched you come, over and over and over again, when I'm ready, lie down. It's time for me to come inside. Kiss you. Taste yourself. Let our scents mingle. I will take you when I'm ready, in my own time, again, and again, and again.

## CONFIDENTIALLY YOURS

### ✳ What He Won't Tell You

You know the difference between a gourmet and a gourmand? The gourmand likes food. The gourmet likes good food. The Bull is a happy combination of both. And to him, there is no such thing as gluttony! It died out in the late Middle Ages. People such as he may be fond of their food, but most people such as he certainly know when to stop. So let's not see any raised eyebrows when he reaches for his third helping of shoofly pie.

And sloth, another deadly sin, is as far from the pure Taurean devotion to economy of energy as lazy is from, say, really lazy. The two have nothing in common. There is Taurean Movement, and there is Taurean Torpor. You can't have one without the other—you've heard of yin and yang—thus Taurean Torpor is a noble state of being, like a personal Black Hole from which future universes belch forth.

Mr. Bull is not stubborn. He is patiently reasonable. His patience is prehistoric; that is, it began before recorded history and will last just as long. Certainly longer than your teeny life span. And his reasonableness is Platonic logic itself—that is, one of the immovable laws of the universe. This is not stubbornness. Is the sun stubborn? The moon? You get the idea.

And if you've ever wondered if someone can carry a grudge through fifteen straight lifetimes without budging an inch, go ahead and insult him. Monsieur does not find it easy to forgive. Forgive? Certainly. He will forgive when he forgets. But since he has unlimited RAM (Random Access Memory) when it comes to personal injury, he never, ever, ever, ever, ever forgets. You've wounded him? You are extinct. You do not exist. You are wiped from the Taurean slate even as the brave but dead matador is carried from the field.

The Bull's cherished habits can become the Bermuda Triangle of routine. Home at 6:00, newspaper at 6:03, TV til 7:28, dinner at 7:29, more TV til 11:01, walk dog at 11:02, brush teeth at 11:26, bed at 11:30. Then we have the Bullster's erotic timetable (see "The Bad Stuff"). His schedule is so boring it could stun an elephant at twenty paces. But the Bull finds such tedium so comforting! Why introduce dangerous variations?

The Bull comprehends money—making it, investing it, watching it grow. A little bird told him he needs to guard it with his life, though. That's the same little bird that sits on his shoulder and yells, "Cheep! Cheep!" at every possible opportunity. Flowers for your date? He picked them himself! Dinner out? Let's take this delicious casserole out behind the garage! Here, he'll spread his sweater down on the concrete. Don't worry about getting it dirty. It hasn't been washed in a year. Oh, and by the way, he made the casserole himself. From leftovers.

Mr. Bull is so possessive that he would gladly breathe for you, and does so upon occasion. This habit, combined with his stupefying penchant for routine, may occasionally make you feel buried alive. If this happens, gently and humorously inform him you think it's healthier if you breathe for yourself, thank you, and furthermore, how about eating dinner tonight *after* the seven o'clock news? You'll give him a massage to stimulate his appetite.

## * The Bad Stuff

Ittle Snookie seepy? Awwwwwww. Snookie go seepy pie? Pookie take Snookie go seepy pie, kay? Kay.

This communication style is especially attractive coming from a large, charitably proportioned, conservative, opinionated male. It's the contrast that makes it so endearing. No? You disagree? Poo-poo on Pookie! Yes, we know Shakespeare was a Taurus, but it was a late birth.

Fond of mountaineering? Roughing it, to the

Bull, means he actually has to press a button to call room service . . . couldn't they have psychics on staff who simply knew that he needed fettuccini Alfredo at 3 A.M.? Don't plan on having the Bull follow you down unexplored black diamond trails on the upper crest. You ski; he'll sit by the fire and mull the wine for the two of you. If he keeps breathing, it qualifies as aerobic activity.

You've heard of paint-by-the-numbers? The Bull has sex-by-the-numbers.

1. neck kiss
2. ear nibble
3. mouth kiss
3a. slight tongue
3b. more tongue
3c. serious tongue
3d. withdraw tongue
4. proceed down neck
4a. stop at collarbone; kiss
4b. proceed down chest
4c. stop at sternum
5. kiss left nipple
5a. kiss right nipple
5b. proceed down to navel
5c. sniff navel; kiss.

And so forth. This is his nightly traffic pattern. No need to wonder where he's headed—and it takes all that tiresome guesswork out of copulation.

If you crave impulsive, dazzlingly innovative sex in which you frequently take the lead, *Escaaaaaaappppeee Nowwwwwwwwwwww*!!! Taurus is sensual, *mais oui*. But he is not attuned to the finer nuances of romantic, emotional connection while in bed. Nor does he possess the elusive, airier-than-thou qualities of sexual mysticism that some females crave. But you were tired of all that, anyway. If you're looking for an erotic explorer to take you to the dark side of the moon, check out Scorpio, Aries, or Cancer.

The Bull is sartorially challenged. Wonder what kind of pizza he ordered last night at 2 A.M.? Just taste his pajamas. Don't worry about fashion sense, the Bull snorts at such airy-fairy concepts. He'd rather be naked anyway. That's why there are holes in his sweaters and he wears ancient, see-through sneakers. It's as close as he can get to Mother Nature.

Do NOT hold your breath as you wait for him to admit he's made a mistake. Besides, it was not his fault. The Bull is sorry "*that*"—that you're upset, that he's upset, that his appetite is ruined. He is not sorry "for" anything. You could possibly tease and cuddle him into a good mood after he's grievously offended you. This qualifies as his forgiving you for noticing that something is wrong. This is as far as he goes. Hope you're adaptable.

P.S.—Are you New Age? Keep it a secret. Never offer him carrot juice. Hide the Tarot cards. And this book! The Bull is appalled that people actually make life decisions according to this nonsense.

## ✴ How Taurus Likes His Women

Barefoot and pregnant. Oops! Wrong category! See "The Bad Stuff." Meanwhile, he likes you sensual, comforting, and down-to-earth with a special kind of dignity that's all your own. You are marvelously sensible; you know how to plant a vegetable garden in spring, and you preserve your own peaches. Taurus is Elementally Male, like iron ore. There-

fore, you are Elementally Female, like the moon
over the eternal tides. And you're wise enough to
revel in the difference. One thing you possess is an
abundance of deep, emotional feeling, which you
graciously share with your Bull at all times. Another thing you possess is the ability to relax. You
really know how to let go, especially behind closed
doors, especially with him.

## ✳ What The Bull Sees When He Looks At You

You like nothing better than to hole up in the
kitchen, baking brioche on a rainy day. Your
kitchen is a masterpiece of equipment, and
your greatest joy would be to cook dinner with
your Bull, sipping a little wine, making a little pasta
and sneaking a little nooky as the rain gently falls
on the roof. Yet how well you deal with the outside
world! You are not the tie-dyed Earth Mother type,
but coolly and practically interested in solid mutual
funds, NASDAQ, and foreign currency. Furthermore, you dress beautifully, in soft, luxurious
clothes that feel fabulous to the touch. And while
you have a drawerful of Naughty Nighties to enhance his visual pleasure, you neither flaunt nor
flirt with other men.

## ✳ What Turns Him On

You know the really nice, dependable guy who's
not a bastard and not flashy and is the one you
should really marry instead of the darkly abusive,
sexual water rat you've been shtupping on some
warehouse floor? Look no further. This is he. This
is a wonderful man—for the right woman. So to
turn him on, be reserved but friendly. Do not pour
out your heart or your troubles to this man until a

year after the wedding. Do not come all cluttered up with hordes of admirers. Get to know him. He needs to be learned and gently known; it makes you real to him. And do NOT hide your sensuality! The way you move, the way you eat, the way you use your hands when you listen to him—he will be watching with invisible sensors to see if you can match his fathomless, fabulous appetites.

## ✳ What Rules The Bull

French mothers do not tell their children to be good. How common. They tell them to be reasonable. *"Sois raisonnable, cherie,"* they say. All French mothers are Taureans at heart. Taurus may be ruled by Venus, but he lives according to a practical, logical reasoning that gets him everything he wants. Life is usually plain and simple to the Bull. And when it isn't, he digs in his heels until it is.

# THE CHASE

## ✳ His Secret Paradox

The Bull is WYSIWYG (wizzy-wig): What You See Is What You Get. His paradoxes, like the rest of him, are simple. On the outside, he's plodding, sensible, hard-working, conservative, old-fashioned, and anachronistic. On the inside, he's Mr. Moo, a cuddly lump of affection who melts in your mouth. Not to mention other places.

A real paradox, however, is that this bosom buddy can exhibit a real depressive streak once in a while, complete with navel-gazing and gloomy thoughts that would put Pisces to shame. How to get him out of one of these? Let him sniff your homemade pot roast and tickle him until he falls out of his chair.

## * How To Bewitch Taurus

Anything worth having is worth striving for, said your grandfather. True? Taurus certainly thinks so. Translated, this means *you don't come cheap.* Remember he willingly expects to toil patiently for what he wants. If you're that easy, there must be something wrong.

So remember that Value is the Bull's middle name. Like Capricorn, if there's no price tag, he doesn't get it. Your price tag is hours and hours of his patient efforts to court you and keep you. You, with your sweetly practical nature and wonderful good manners. All this will send red-alert signals to the well-developed "mate" section in the Bull's brain, and he will begin to train his sights on you.

Do not bewitch this man if you don't want him. He's serious about marriage, and he will literally spend years coming after you, or pining for you, or mourning you, or trying to make you into a friend. Besides, imagine what it's like to be stalked everywhere you go by an aircraft carrier. Unless you're both out for a fling, don't toy with his affections. If you rouse his sleeping rage, you will need a rest home to recover.

## * Don't . . .

Bother being subtle. Tell him what the Tarot said about him. Tell him you always defend him to your family, and who needs a reputation anyway? Use the word "stubborn" in an argument. Tease him—look what happens to matadors who do this once too often. Call him "smoochums" in public. Flirt openly with other men. Serve him leftover scrambled eggs for dinner. Have green things growing on the milk carton in your refrigerator. Clean the attic without warning.

## ✳ Who He Likes To Bed

Mother Nature herself, in all her naked glory. The Bull's sensuality is infinite; he can get lost just staring at you, feeling you with his extrasensory fingertips, or contemplating a strand of your hair. He likes a woman who matches his gargantuan, earthy appetites—someone who would love to spend Thanksgiving holiday in bed, reaching the occasional languid hand for more champagne and stuffing. A cozy, unaffected woman who lies in wait for him underneath mountains of down quilts, where she becomes both his heart's desire and his journey's end, every night for the rest of his life.

## ✳ Who He Likes To Wed

June Cleaver. But a June Cleaver with the appetites of Sophia Loren, who wouldn't mind making love in a huge vat of spaghetti. He's looking. He's definitely looking. The Bull needs the stability of marriage both for the emotional security it provides and because being wrapped in a warm, toasty, faithful love is part of his purpose in life.

P.S.—The Bull is the last word in strong and steady husbands: he's accountabull, reliabull, responsibull, capabull, and dependabull. He likes nothing better than to be your rod and your staff (especially your rod) as Life's storms swirl on by.

## * What He's Secretly Afraid Of

If he looks in the mirror he might see Jabba the
Hutt. What if the currency devalued and the market crashed and gold hit a new low and bonds were
unstable? What if he were out on some street corner, in the rain, with his faithful dog, who had the
flu, and they were—gad!—*panhandling*? Women
prefer men who make sparkling repartee. Women
prefer men with low fat ratios.

## * When To Say Yes

With Taurus, you will both know when to say yes.
This is because he will come after you so relentlessly that you have either escaped in terror to the
North Pole, or you have surrendered utterly and
welcomed him with open, voluptuous arms. Since
he is shy and will take his time, by the time the
Moment has arrived, You Will Know. In much the
same way that (if you've seen *Jurassic Park*) you can
tell the *Tyrannosaurus rex* is approaching by the
subtle rattling of your coffee cup, You Will Know.

# THE COUP DE GRACE

## * His Sexual Secrets And Desires

The way to a man's heart is through his stomach.
In the Bull's case, it's also the way to his brain and
other vital organs. This is one lusty, erotic animal.
His sense of touch is awesome. He's kinesthetic to
his toes. His appetite is gargantuan, and the best
part is . . . he takes his time. So target every one of
his five senses for meltdown.

The Bull prefers nightly sports to take place in
the bedroom, where they belong. And setting is

very, very important to this man. Have soft, sexy
music in the background, and use aromatic oil on
the lightbulbs to perfume the air. Put satin sheets
on the bed. Invest in pillows—a dozen, at least—
and be sure they're soft, floppy, and inviting. If you
have a king-size bed, bravo! Taurus feels most at
home in huge surroundings. A vase or two of flowers will warm his eye, and they can come in useful
later.

Lay in a few bottles of his favorite wine and
brandy, and a chilled bottle or two of Mumm's.
Prepare a feast fit for an emperor (Taureans make
very good emperors). What to serve? Anthing that
can be eaten with the fingers. Chilled shrimp with
spicy sauce, crab sticks, whole fresh peaches,
smoked chicken in Thai peanut sauce, chocolate
buttercream truffles, white chocolate tarts with
Grand Marnier icing . . . food as sex. You get the
idea.

When he opens the door, a little note tells him to
take off his shoes and socks and proceed to the
couch. When he gets to the couch, another note in-
structs him to remove his shirt and jacket. There's
a glass of champagne and directions to proceed to
the kitchen. There he is to remove the rest of his
clothes and take the picnic tray into the bedroom.

Where are you? You are naked, gloriously naked,
just as he prefers you, amid a nest of pillows in soft
candlelight, waiting. You have placed a chocolate
truffle on each breast. Invite him to sample you.
Then it's his turn to lie back on the cushions. Place
a black velvet blindfold over his eyes. Gently stroke
one of his special places with a flower. Tell him he
has to guess what kind it is. A wrong guess, and
he gets a nibble of dinner. A right guess, and he
gets a nibble of you—any part he requests. Take

this seriously! Taurus has an incredible sense of touch, and he loves to be stroked by the hour.

Tell him you have a dozen kinds of flowers, and he has to guess them all before he comes tonight. He'll won't be able to hear you—he's in nirvana.

## * Shhh . . .

Let your Bull seduce you sometime when you've been working in the garden or cooking up a storm. Let him experience you *au naturel*, and give over to his extraordinary sensuality. He'll go crazy. Don't be shy. He adores your Provençal cooking. Why shouldn't he adore you?

## AFTERGLOW: WHAT YOU NEED TO KNOW

### * What Taurus Likes Better Than Sex

Food. No, we didn't really mean that. Security wins by a hair. Security means money to Taurus; it means that he can lock the front door some day and throw away the key, retiring happily behind the walls of his snug, well-stocked fortress. However, don't let his prudence rain on your parade. Remind him that life is to be lived, not saved for.

### * Will He Marry His Best Lover Or Best Friend?

He really wants a perfect blend of both. The Bull turns all his ex-lovers into friends. He can't help it. For him there is no dividing line. He will marry his sensuous, earthy companion who has captured his great, shy heart and he will remain her Rock of Gibraltar from that day forth.

### * What He Wants From You

Affection, in large gulps. Hugs, strokes, little pal-
pations, squeezes, the 7:05 embrace, the 8:12 embrace, the 9:16 embrace. Massages. Foot rubs, back
rubs, tiny kisses on his chest fur. Nookies, noshes,
chocolate kisses in all shapes and sizes. Mouth-to-
mouth resuscitation, daily. This will dissolve the
tough Taurean hide into maple syrup in no time.

### * What He Needs From You

He is the immovable plaque. Be the irresistible
force. Shower him with all the magic of your heart,
in every conceivable form: love, passion, affection,
kindness, solid friendship, esteem, respect, fond-
ness, warmth, tenderness and desire. The heart is
the only country where the Bull feels a bit timid,
and he needs a loving guide to show him how to
make his home there. Besides, he needs to know
that he's perfect all by himself, and that all the
world's opinions don't matter a damn—to you or
to him.

### * What He Won't Give Up For You

His bank balance. His opinions, right or wrong. His
love of God, country, and waterbed. His custom-
built refrigerator. His burdens of responsibility,
which he carries with dignity. His habit of having
tiny, invisible crushes on friends and strangers. All
that important junk in the garage.

### * What He Will Give Up For You

Taurus does not give up, as in "let go of," anything.
Let GO? Of his possessions? His memories? His ac-
quisitions? His collections? What, exactly, does this

phrase mean? He's never heard of it. You are the ultimate collectible that he has persevered to acquire; you are the jewel in his domestic crown. No serious collector *gives up* anything—that's not the idea here. What exotic notions you have! Are you sure you're a Republican?

## * How To Make Him Fall In Love With You, Really

The Bull will never ask for the love and warmth he secretly longs for. So introduce him, slowly, to the infinite colors of the heart, and watch him bloom. When he is loved, truly loved just for his secret, shy, somewhat lonely self, he can at last open up the Great Wall of China that surrounds his ribcage and pour forth his longings, his feelings, and his hopes. He finally feels emotionally secure. And when Taurus feels emotionally secure, he quietly, happily makes his dreams come true. And never forget: this man's dreams are worth waiting for.

## * Make It Forever

Let him know that you're his, forever and beyond, and he never has to doubt it. The Bull's love endures throughout the ages, growing only deeper with time. He needs to know that the one he has chosen carries the same timeless feelings as he does, and—most important—that she will never, ever leave him.

Don't forget to humor your Bull. Tease and tickle him out of his moods. He cannot be persuaded, but he can definitely be wheedled, and he needs you to do this for him. Don't leave him stewing and snorting in bullish obstinacy—he might turn to stone right there in his BarcaLounger.

# CRUCIAL MINUTIAE

## * What To Feed Taurus

The Bull is deeply fond of perfectly simple foods, perfectly done. Dazzle him with things that take a lot of time in the kitchen: home-baked breads, homemade soups, and salads to help him conserve his waistline. Astonish him with homemade peach ice cream, topped with real peaches over your best meringue. Better yet, invite him into the kitchen with you, to conduct personal taste tests when you've had a glass or two of good burgundy to open the palate. Remember: white truffles at $80 a pound will impress Leo, but not Taurus. He will be more pleased by your loving effort, not your extravagance.

## * How To Take Care Of Your Bull

Taurus is not sickly, but you can take good care of him anyway by giving him deep, slow massages to ease the tension in his neck and shoulders. The Bull loves all the little signs of cozy companionship: his covers turned down at night, his slippers before the fire, tea and lemon for his sore throat, breakfast in bed with his favorite mug. You cannot give him enough of these little attentions, and he will roll over in ecstacy at your thoughtfulness.

## * For His Birthday

A trip to a spa—a spa where he doesn't have to do anything but lie there, while slaves come and massage him, feed him, and peel his grapes. If there's no spa in the neighborhood, hire a masseuse to arrive at his door, to give him a Swedish or shiatsu massage. Make sure you arrive just as it's over, with a picnic basket of foie gras, champagne, home-made bread, fresh strawberries, and German chocolate cake.

Remember that the Bull loves to collect, especially beautiful things. Buy him an original painting—he will appreciate the taste and the investment. Fine earthenware for his table, copper pans for his kitchen, Scottish throws for his couch will make him swell with delight. In all the right places.

○《●》》

# gemini

*David Winstead*
*6-10-63*
*David DeSeree)*
*6-17-58*

## MAY 22 - JUNE 21

### BEST LOVE MATCHES

Gemini & Aries
Gemini & Leo
Gemini & Libra
Gemini & Aquarius

He's witty, he's clever, and he's got a big audience. Take him seriously? He won't let you—he's having too much fun. He's Gemini, the Twins.

## FAMOUS GEMINIS

Bob Dylan, Donald Trump, Clint Eastwood, Mikhail Baryshnikov, Tim Allen, Paul McCartney, Newt Gingrich, Morgan Freeman, Liam Neeson

## I AM

Wondering how long that huge man by the punch bowl is going to keep shoveling cookies into his mouth. Is this a party or a cattle feed? Call the diet

police. No? Too cruel? But I'm not cruel—he is.
He's eaten five bags of cookies so far. It's not a
pretty sight.

You've noticed all these people around me, and
you've concluded I'm the life of the party. You flat-
ter me; if this party had a pulse, it would need
open-heart surgery. Everyone here is too serious by
half. Which half, you're probably asking. Me, too.

I'd rather be elsewhere. I'd usually rather be elsewhere. Where? Don't pin me down with destina-
tions! Just to go is everything. Just to hop on a bus
or a plane and not know where I'll end up—I live
for that feeling. I hate knowing the end of the story.
It spoils everything.

But I adore being in love. I like that marvelous
sensation of falling, just every so lightly falling, a
little bit in love. It's like a sweet, haunting call in
my mind. Too much love, however, and I'm deaf-
ened. I like it light, like the bubbles that dance on
top of champagne. I love the moment when two
people understand, when they don't need words—
it's a music I could listen to forever.

My desire begins in my mind, and it must be
fulfilled there or my brain cells go on strike. One
must respect the rhythms of sex; a long, slow sizzle
leads to the hottest flame.

I've been told I could charm the nose off the
Sphinx. Can't anyone come up with a better meta-
phor than that? Besides, her nose is broken and I'd
never be rude enough to remind her. I've also been
told that I can schmooze my way around rules and
regulations. So? Wouldn't you? I've always thought
schmoozing should be registered as a lethal
weapon, but then, not everyone schmoozes like I
do.

Is there someone who can dazzle me forever? I

doubt it, but I'd love for you to try! Are you interested, by any chance? You're probably a little bored with your nine-to-five life, aren't you? And that nine-to-five guy you've been seeing? Oh, he's responsible, and accountable, and reliable, and you cook him celery casseroles and all of a sudden you realize your entire life is celery—serious celery.

Am I good for you? Oh, honey, I'm good for the part of you that you buried a long time ago when your mama told you never to trust men like me. You don't know how good.

Not that I'm not responsible. I have a job. I'm good at it. I'm the picture of stability just at the moment. Tomorrow I won't vouch for. But I make magic from words and ideas, and I'll show you how. I can weave a cat's cradle of thought around your head to catch your dreams as they come out. What if your life had a looking glass, like Alice in Wonderland, and you just stepped through it?

So what'll it be, beautiful? Celery? Or Magic?

## YOU ARE

Interested in me because your mind works faster than most of your compadres, and because you hate being so bored much of the time. You think it's socially rude, but what can you do? So what's the antidote? Me!

You are not interested in sex for its own sake. That sort of thing was done by D.H. Lawrence, and you read him when you were ten. There is a kind of courtship between a man and a woman that is like spinning straw into gold; it begins and ends in the mind. Just to make dinner with you is to make wonderful love.

You're smart—you could be smarter than I am—

but that thrills me. I may be restless, but I will
never be bored when you're around. You hate routine as much as I do. The flower that blooms by the
kitchen window never blooms the same way twice
in your eyes.

You have a marvelous practicality about you that
delights me. If you were kidnapped, you would im-
provise an SOS signal with your makeup mirror.
What is out of the ordinary is the stuff of life to
you. You love to analyze relationships. You live for
excellent conversation.

You're looking for someone to make life interesting, to keep up with you, and most important,
not to be threatened by your strength and intelligence. How did I know? I've been looking for you
for most of my life.

## HOW TO DRIVE ME WILD

Keep me guessing. Make me chase you. And
please—never tell me where we're going!

I like love to start in the mind, where all the best
things begin. So don't even speak at first. I like that.
Hold the image of me you want in your mind, and
then talk to me. . . . See if I can pick up on it. When
I pick up on it, change it. When I pick up on that,
change it again. When you start to come after me,
do it with words first. Make it subtle. Keep me
guessing. When I think you're interested, disappear
for a little. Just a little. You can stay in the room,
but just . . . disappear. The longer you tantalize me,
the hotter I will be for you.

When you think it's right, show me your idea of
romance. Show me the sea, or the mountains, or
candlelight, or a fire . . . share your romantic
thoughts with me. Discover what my secret idea of

romance is. I won't tell you at first. See if you can guess. The first time you kiss me, make it light, as if a sea breeze had just passed between us.

Take me somewhere different, somewhere unknown to me. Romance is important. Urgently important. Kiss me. No, talk to me while you're kissing me . . . I love that . . . see how long we can keep it up before we succumb to wilder passions.

When I touch you, I want to know that I have found someone who broke through my barriers and found out my secrets. I want to be understood. I don't understand myself, but in knowing you I want to feel known. Do you know how kindling burns, quickly and lightly, before the roar of the real fire? Let your kisses be kindling. Kiss my face, my hair, my throat; let your mouth drift over my chest and my arms. Hold back just a little; read me a line of that poem you brought while you kiss my forehead.

Now stop. Stand up. Take off the rest of your clothes. NO! Don't blow out the candle—light another one. Turn slowly so I can see you from all angles. Look at me while I watch you. Ask me questions. Ask me if I want you. Ask me *how* I want you. Now walk over to me and sit where my mouth can reach you. Pick up your book of poetry. Read to me while I try to distract you with my tongue. Keep reading. See how long you can keep going before you give in to me. To us. To the night. That was lovely. . . . Now it's my turn.

## CONFIDENTIALLY YOURS

### ✶ What He Won't Tell You

He'd like to make up his mind. He just doesn't know how. You've heard that Gemini is two people, but you don't know what this means.

It means that now you see him, now you don't. And he's still standing there! Even when he decides on one persona and sticks to it, he still has a shadow that watches everything he does. He can't get free of it. There'll always be the three of you in bed: you, Gemini, and the Watcher in the back of his head.

Does he love you with his whole soul, his whole heart, and his whole mind? Don't worry—he has a spare set you'll never lay eyes on. Don't even bother asking him where he is while he's gazing deep into your eyes—to Gemini, daydreaming is a sacred art, to be practiced in secret and alone.

The Gemster is the ultimate tourist. He doesn't linger, he doesn't stick around, he doesn't commit. He is life's supreme visitor. Even the most stable-looking Geminis have nine times nine irons in the fire, just to keep things flowing. If people were paid to taste-test life, Geminis would make a mint.

That's why the word "commitment" makes him break out in a rash. If you can see a thousand sides to every question, how can you commit to an answer? Much less a person? Besides, in order to commit, you have to be stable, reliable, responsible, and adult—all those things they didn't teach him in Never-Never Land. Poor Gemster.

In self-defense, he's had to develop the quickest exit lines in the zodiac. So when you notice him fleeing out the back door just as you were making plans for next week, console yourself with the thought that he's just being true to his two-faced self. Besides, he's the most charming drifter you will ever say good-bye to. He'll have you lending him money for bus fare as he borrows your phone to call his "sister" in the next state. And he'll make you feel glad just to help him along his way.

Mr. Twin likes to bypass the old heart valve in favor of a love connection that he has more control over—i.e., the brain. Gemini isn't comfortable with deep wells of feeling. Nasty people would say that it's because he doesn't have any.

Gemini is Mr. Broadcast News. Never confide something you don't want repeated. He's verbal, analytical, and linguistically dazzling. He badly needs to feel, instead of think, but feelings are harder to deconstruct than word games, so who needs 'em? Besides, maybe a thought is a feeling (no one's proved it isn't!). So therefore he's in total touch with his thoughts, er, feelings, so therefore he doesn't have a problem knowing what he's thinking, uh, feeling. This is a tidbit of glorious Gemini doublespeak. And if you're involved with one, you'll be hearing a lot more.

## ✳ The Bad Stuff

I schmooze, therefore I am.

So now that he's spent months pursuing you, charming you into giving up your sheltered, modest little life and flying away with him straight to Never-Never Land—does he really want you? Sure. Maybe. He thought he did. Were you worth the effort? Yeah, probably. Why not? You weren't actually planning to *live* with him for the rest of your life though, were you? Oh dear! Because he didn't mean *that!* "Happily ever after" is just a phrase! A sweet nothing! Words are magical, aren't they? Don't you have a job to go back to?

Shallow? Gemini has the emotional depth of a rain puddle. No need to worry about drowning in the dark seas of his soul—just pull on your rubbers and splash away. He could develop depth, but that would require willpower, which is the death of spontaneity, which is why he doesn't have any.

Gemini's relationship to the Truth is too holy and mystical to explain. This is worse than it sounds. Never press him for the truth, the whole truth, and nothing but the truth—you'll give him a nervous breakdown.

Cold? Gemini could probably stay alive on Mars, where it's 200 degrees below Fahrenheit. Is that a heart or a freezer in his chest? Well, he wasn't utilizing his heart much, so why not shove it aside and make room for something really functional? There's Gemini practicality for you!

Does Mr. Twin kiss and tell? You betcha! To avoid becoming gossip fodder, don't give in to this man unless he's serious. That means: he's on his way up the aisle to the altar and the honeymoon suite has been paid for—in cash.

And don't argue with him. You will be verbalized to death—a sad ending for beautiful, postfeminist creature like yourself. Either that or you will be so angry at the nuclear-powered barrage of words coming at you, you will engage in battle just for the sheer satisfaction of getting him to shut up, *which will never happen*. He must win arguments or die, and he will talk you into a coma in order to do so. The Gemster doesn't take kindly to defeat. It smells uncomfortably like failure, a condition that haunts him and might possibly, he believes, turn him to stone.

Gemini has trouble internalizing achievement— he's never quite sure if he got the job on performance or charm. Since his charm is positively awesome, this is not a trivial question, thus his continued need to keep winning, charming, fascinating, and intriguing his audience—you. He's tap dancing on the high wire, and while it's a mesmerizing act, he's rather afraid that underneath the razzle-dazzle, there's nothing there.

## ✳ How Gemini Likes His Women

Smart and sane. As with Aquarius, women are not the end-all and be-all of this man's existence. He likes to be amused, baffled, and kept off balance. Gemini likes nice girls who become strong, independent women. And he loves a woman who has integrated her brains and her femininity.

So, you are witty. Even-tempered. Cheerful. If you are one of those Poets of the Dark Side, one who dwells in melancholy and midnight moods, if the woods you love are dark and deep, flee! Flee! Gemini despises melancholy, tristesse, introspection, and the dark side of life. Like, hey, dude, what a downer!

Beware: men fall in love with what they see; women with what they hear. And the Gemster knows, oh, just exactly what you've always longed to hear from a man. He's got that perfect-pitch verbal blend of wit, challenge, and enchantment, and—*watch out!* He'll weave a spell of words so dazzling that you'll be lost in an enchanted forest and confuse the fog of his charm for solid ground. So don't give up anything for him until you have a guarantee. And remember—it's not love; it's fog. Think fog.

## ✳ What The Twin Sees When He Looks At You

Remember the Breck shampoo girls? Those dazzlingly clean emblems of the middle class on the back of every magazine? Gemini likes a modern

version of Ms. Breck. You got straight A's, you
were president of all the clubs, you're maybe a little
too brainy for your own good, and you thought
winning all those Girl Scout badges was peachy-
keen fun. You probably still wear kilts and knee
socks—and on you, they look sexy. Your hair is
perfectly cut, you brush your teeth three times a
day, and you look marvelous in a beret with a little
pin on the side.

## ✳ What Turns Him On

The unpredictable. Not knowing if you really want
him or not. Not knowing what you're hiding up
your sleeve. The biggest turn-on of all, however, is
your mind. This is one guy who sure ain't threatened by brains. So go ahead—be as smart as you've
always wanted to be in front of another human being. He can't get enough. You're looking for an
equal, not a master, and Gemini is looking for you.

## ✳ What Rules The Twins

Restlessness. A genetically induced need to see if
the grass is greener over in the next time zone.
Gemini is always just one mental step ahead, or to
the side, or above where you think he'll be. If he
stays in one place too long, his brain heats up to
overdrive and he explodes. So, you see, he has to
keep moving. Make sure you enjoy travel—all
kinds—if you want to stick around.

# THE CHASE

## ✳ His Secret Paradox

He wants to be externally stimulated without cease,
but he longs for his inner delirium to stop. He

would like, some day, to encounter peace. But it stops for Gemini only when he is so immersed in something that he forgets himself—when he has what is called the "Flow experience." In Gemini's case, this is a rare and truly beautiful event to behold. If you can give him this serene encounter, he will be yours for life.

### * How To Bewitch Gemini

Don't give in. Don't even let on that he's getting to you at all. Let him assume, presume, and conjecture until he's got dry-mouth trying to coax you into his arms. He's magnetized by chance, the odds, the throw of the dice. Maybe you care; maybe you don't. Maybe it depends on what you ate for breakfast? He's riveted. It stimulates those high-frequency antennae attached to his forehead. (You can't see them? They're there.)

And by all means, keep something to yourself! You are in danger of falling in love with someone who is twisting himself into a human pretzel to fall in love with you, and when it's finally happened, he will mumble under his breath, "So what's next?" *Teach him that there is no next—at least, not without you.*

Psst! The Gemster can be fun. Really fun. He's light, he's romantic, he's in the mood—in fact, he *is* the mood, most of the time. Don't fall head over heels before he does, though, or you may be in for a bumpy ride.

### * Don't . . .

Schedule sex. Ask him if he's heard of a savings account. Ask him what he's actually *doing* with his life. Suggest that he manage your money. Let him see your money. Hint that you have money. Invite him to go shopping. Light black candles and listen to Leonard Cohen a lot. Tell shaggy-dog stories. Invite him to spend the weekend digging in the garden. Tell him what you plan to be doing every day for the next three years.

## ✳ Who He Likes To Bed

Tinkerbell, with a decent IQ. An airy, witty female who piques his interest and whom he can't catch all that easily. Gemini is not seduced by a heavy come-on, by salty, primitive sexuality, or by heart-throbbing romance. He likes to be teased, intrigued, and amused. He especially likes it if you can convey that the sexual act is a delicious detour to your main goal, which is some wonderful game between the two of you. If this sounds obscure, it is! Obscure, fascinating plots and machinations are just what Gemini craves.

Gemini is not riveted by the ancient male/female dance of desire. He can, in fact, get kinda bored by the typical female come-on game. To be sure you distinguish yourself from the crowd, don't even try to seduce him. Challenge him to an acrostics puzzle, or the latest CD-ROM computer game. Pretend to ignore your biological differences. Let it begin to dawn on him.

## ✳ Who He Likes To Wed

Um, he doesn't. He understands the value of marriage as a social institution; just be sure to leave him out, thank you very much. After a few decades, however, and if he really has to, he will settle down with a clever, amusing, impetuous girl, who adores adventure and won't crowd him with too much emotion or deep talks about The Relationship. Assuming she has been smart enough to surprise the hell out of him by becoming the only woman in the world who understands him—i.e., the woman he loves.

## ✱ What He's Secretly Afraid Of

He's no stud-puppy. When he stares deep into the well of his soul, the Roadrunner stares back. It's not dazzling mental acuity; it's a panic attack. Man cannot live by nerves alone. Habit is the cornerstone of a well-lived life. Actually, true freedom is not detachment from all human feeling. There's an inverse ratio between charm and achievement. Women prefer darkly sexual, primitive men. He's succeeded by his charm alone.

## ✱ When To Say Yes

Long, oh, long after you'd say yes to other signs. This guy really likes to spin it out. Spinning it out can have its advantages—he likes romance and mood as much as you do. However, if you have marriage in mind, *wait until he's become a grown-up!* As with the Aries male, you wouldn't want to endure his first thirty-odd years anyway, with the restless, casual, relentlessly changing scene that he needs in order to keep himself stimulated.

## THE COUP DE GRACE

## ✱ His Sexual Secrets And Desires

Gemini is majorly visual. Have mirrors set up so the Watcher can watch himself watching you. He'll be deeply thrilled. By all means, keeps the lights on. But let the lighting be subtle enough to cast a spell of romance over the two of you. Romance has profound significance for Gemini. Buy some elegant lingerie—a pure cotton nightdress, a woven silk robe. Be suggestive, graceful, romantic, and conceal just enough to rivet his visual attention.

Gemini likes things to begin way before they begin. He's imaginative and romantic, and mood is as important to him as it is to you. He also likes experimentation and surprises. Invite him to a party. Show up at his door in a stunning dress. Ask him if he's ever seen those little plastic egg-shaped vibrators that fit snugly into the vagina and can be buzzed by remote control. Tell him that the man has all the control in that situation, and that the woman is hopelessly aroused whenever he presses the button. Now proceed to the party. When you walk in the door, mention that you forgot to wear underwear. Wait until he's ensconced himself in the center of an admiring crowd. Then slide up and hand him a buzzer.

This little trick should rivet his erotic attention with masterful precision. Let him see the effects of his toy, but discreetly. Only the two of you will know what you're doing. Meanwhile, continue to tease him and do not stop talking.

Undoubtedly, you will leave that party early. When you have reached your bedroom, light the candles you've placed around the bed. Make sure there are several mirrors, and they are all facing the right direction. Pour some champagne and talk to him, while he's kissing you. Ask him to tell you his most erotic fantasy. Refuse to touch him unless he keeps talking—he can do both at once, never fear.

Now stand in front of the mirrors, while you slowly, *slowly*, strip off your dress. Be sure you're wearing a drop-dead bra or teddy. Tell him you didn't think that fantasy was his most erotic. Tell him you won't go any farther unless he tells you the truth. If he protests, tell him you're sure he can think of something more outrageous.

Slowly slip out of your teddy. If he stops talking, stop stripping. Now climb onto the bed and lightly, lightly caress him with two long feathers. Start with his feet. Ask him to spread his legs so you can use the feathers over his balls. Linger over his penis, and see if you can make the feathers dance with the pulse of his hard-on. Ask him if he wants to play a game. When he says yes, ask him how much. Graze his thighs and balls while you ask. Ask him again, using a feather. Does he really want to play? Slip the feather up and over the tip of his penis, back and forth, back and forth. Ask him if he's willing to wear a mask. Browse up and down his penis while you ask. Tell him he can't play if he won't.

When he says yes, show him two black silk masks. Slip one over his eyes and one over yours. Then sit lightly and gently down on his erect penis. Kiss him. Tell him all's fair in love and war. Now tell him that the last person who comes, wins.

### ✳ Shhh . . .

Make a video of the two of you together (hide the camera in a slightly open closet). Mark the tape "Confidential," and send it to him at work.

## AFTERGLOW: WHAT YOU NEED TO KNOW

### ✳ What Gemini Likes Better Than Sex

Verbalizing! The man has to communicate or he will explode. Never forget to convey, disclose, discuss, and commune with your Gemini, and he will be will yours forever and a day.

## ✳ Will He Marry His Best Lover Or Best Friend?

He will marry his beloved companion, she who understands him to the max, she who gives him "space," who stimulates him, who's as smart as he is in her own delightful way, who aches for adventure, and to whom romance and magic are (shhh!) more important than mere sex.

## ✳ What He Wants From You

Stimulation. Surprises. Entertainment. Freedom. The more multifaceted you are, the better. Don't hold back when it comes to pursuing your own interests—let him tag along and be fascinated.

## ✳ What He Needs From You

Understanding. Mr. Twin can choke to death on his own logic. Listen to him—really, really listen, as if your life depended on it. Gemini needs you— although he doesn't know it—to help make his dreams come true. With your profound understanding of who he really is, he can finally see himself as he always wanted to be. Where? In your eyes. Hold that image of him close to your heart, and he will stick around forever and make it all come true.

## ✳ What He Won't Give Up For You

His craving to see what's on the other side of the wall, door, room, job, country, hemisphere. His favorite games. His need to amuse, to charm, to schmooze, to dazzle. If there's no audience, Gemini will create one. And never ask him to stop flirting—that would be like cutting off his blood supply.

## ✳ What He Will Give Up For You

If you're really the one who can Understand Him—no mean feat—he will give up looking over his shoulder to see who he's missing while he's busy kissing you. He will, in fact, be astonished that you, the one who really, truly, understands, exist. He thought you didn't.

## ✳ How To Make Him Fall In Love With You, Really

*Step One:* Take your time. Take lots of time. Let him see inch by inch that you're always there, tuned in to his many dozens of frequencies, and that it's all understood. Keep enough distance so that he has to reach out for you—just give him a little room to chase here and there, even after you're married.

*Step Two:* Listen to him. Just listen, endlessly. He'll be delighted, then puzzled, then seriously interested, then amazed. This is one sign that needs to be tamed. How do you tame him? Attend to his words. Carefully.

*Step Three:* He needs to learn how to feel. Mr. Twin's heart is barely used, making it ripe for development in a loving, careful manner. And his brain could use a rest, as he himself would testify if he were being honest. Allow him to see how comfortable you are with your feelings, how nonthreatening they can be. Acknowledge him when he has one. Tell him he has just had a feeling, if need be, and how safe that was. See! They don't bite! Why, he barely even felt it! Why not have another one?

*Step Four:* Love him. Simply, completely, just as he is, not as he might be. Don't stop.

## ✳ Make It Forever

Mr. G is the eternal watcher; this is a guy who observed the obstetrician's technique while he was being born. What Gemini wants, more than anything, is to forget himself. He wants the "Flow experience," and while "Flow" may be a piece of cake for Pisces, it is very hard for the Gemini man to lose himself in anything—even you.

So give him the unheard-of experience of unconditional understanding. He has never felt completely understood in his life, right down to his toes, and being unconditionally understood will be close to a religious experience for him. In fact, it will make him come back. If he's crazy about you on Tuesday, by Friday he's disappeared. But don't freak, don't let on, and don't fight it. Let him go. He'll circle around again, just to see how you're taking it. Let him. And make sure that every time he comes around, it's safe, and relaxing, and fun, and he's understood.

Some men fall in love and stay there. Gemini flies in and out of love a dozen times a day. The thing to do is imprint the love experience on his brain so that it becomes his only reality. This is done by subtle reinforcement, over and over, until he caves in. This is not cheating. You have his best interests at heart—loving you.

# CRUCIAL MINUTIAE

## ✳ What To Feed Gemini

Geminis will try anything—twice. Thai, Chinese, French, Hawaiian, Russian, anything and everything in between will delight this man as you take him to new places and discover new taste sensations. But don't neglect his nerves. Soothing teas, homemade soup, country breads—all these will calm your Gemini and help his body relax. True relaxation is not easy for Mr. Twin, so be sure to include foods like turkey and warm milk, which contain lots of tryptophan and will calm him down considerably.

Psst! Geminis we have known have all had a secret yen for Mom's home cooking. So send him a basket of homemade blueberry muffins for breakfast. Make him all your specialties—especially if they are simple, homegrown recipes like chicken pot pie, oatmeal with raisins, and peanut butter and jelly sandwiches. He will blush with pleasure. Inside.

## ✳ How To Take Care Of Your Gem

Nurse those nerves! Gemini has a fragile mental ecosystem—he's not what you'd call "grounded" a lot of the time. Introduce him to the subtle powers of massage on a regular basis. Be sure to have music to keep the first few tracks of his mind occupied while you concentrate on the rest of him. Try water music, natural sounds, or a wandering flute—anything to get his mind to slow from warp speed down to a more manageable level. Have books all over the place—Geminis love to read, and books reassure them that all's right with the world. Unlike

Taurus, Gemini does not get lost in sensuality. However, one perfect cashmere blanket to wrap him in in winter, one exquisite rose at the breakfast table—anything that contains a surprise, a thought, an idea—will delight and astound him.

## * For His Birthday

Definitely take him someplace out of the ordinary and DO NOT tell him where you're going. Not knowing what's around the corner is pure catnip to a Gemini guy. What's out of the ordinary? The zoo, the circus, indoor skiing, hot-air ballooning, rock climbing, a crawfish festival, the soapbox derby, even the local park, where you can have a picnic on the swings—which he probably hasn't laid eyes on in twenty years. Geminis are usually bright, so a museum should light up his eyes, or a lecture on anything from the Illuminati to chaos theory. Also, don't neglect the newest computer games, electronic checkbooks, the Internet, or a TV-watch. Finally, when all else fails, go for books! Geminis are bookworms, and the more imaginative the read, the better he'll like it.

# ☽☾●☽☽

# cancer

## JUNE 22 - JULY 23

### BEST LOVE MATCHES

Cancer & Taurus
Cancer & Leo
Cancer & Scorpio
Cancer & Pisces

He's the center of a small crowd, and he's holding them spellbound with his stories. He's funny. He's deep. He's a first-class romantic. He's quietly running the show. He's Cancer, the Crab.

### FAMOUS CANCERIANS:

Bill Cosby, Tom Cruise, Bill Blass, Sylvester Stallone, Chris O'Donnell, Giorgio Armani, Anthony Edwards, H. Ross Perot, Harrison Ford, Jimmy Smits

## I AM

Shy. Although you are beautiful, I would never lunge across a room toward the woman I desire. It's not my style. Besides, I can tell that's not what you'd prefer. I possess a highly developed intuition. And yet I am very male. Have you ever known a sensual, aggressive man who understood the importance of shopping? Who understood why you need five pairs of turquoise sandals? Who cried along with you while watching *Gone with the Wind*? I thought not. You can't hide from me the way you're used to hiding from men; I have radar no one else has ever bothered to notice, let alone develop.

I have been called fussy, but I resent this. I do not fuss; I take infinite, meticulous care. Particularly when I am passionate about something—and I am always passionate. My custom-built, climate-controlled picnic basket should demonstrate this. When I am lying under the linden tree gazing into your eyes, I do not want to drink room-temperature champagne. What a waste of mood! And I give very, very good mood.

I understand money as well as I will soon understand you, but don't let this frighten you. I enjoy building a strong, comfortable nest around my loved ones, to keep them happily safe and secure ever after. Loved ones? Plural? But children are the flowers of a great love, and I will have a great love or I will have nothing at all. I think we need at least three kids, don't you?

I sound desperately serious. I don't usually lecture people, only beautiful witty women who intimidate me. That was a joke. Why not steal away from this desperately chic affair with its bad wine and trendoid food—I mean if you eat too much goat-cheese pizza you might start to bleat—and meet me for an ice cream soda somewhere? Will you come? I'd like to get to know you.

By the way, whoever told you I was into control? They were raving! I manage other people's lives for them as a favor. Besides, I do it in such an unobtrusive, low-profile way. Most people could benefit from a little executive supervision, particularly as long as they never know. I think of it as my personal service to mankind.

I will come for you in a thousand ways before I come for you. I will know that the way you wear your favorite sweater is a message to the world; I will know how you're feeling by how much makeup you've decided to put on that day; I will receive the tiny unsent messages that tell me that you don't like to be overwhelmed by kisses, that you prefer to taste my lips slowly, not too much. Let there be time and thoughts between our lips. Let me court you. Courting a woman is a high art, and I am a master at it. I am very aggressive, but in a persistent, polished, tenacious way. And I am very, very patient. Think about that.

I must lead, but I must be *allowed* to lead. Romance is a two-step, and I want you there beside me for every intricate turn in the dance. I want to make love *with* you, my dear, not to you, and there is a world of difference between those two little words.

## YOU ARE

The angel on top of the Christmas tree. You are special, a standout in some quietly extraordinary way. You are not lewd, aggressive, or overpowering. You have a slightly old-fashioned sense about you that is absolutely delightful.

I've been told I expect far too much. Ridiculous! There is a perfect woman somewhere, and I will not rest until I find you. You have a softness about you that drives me wild. While you may have nights of wild abandon in your eyes, or be the fiercest litigator in the firm, there is a lingering aura of softness that slowly melts my heart. The girl in you is never far from the surface, and I see her in your face whenever I'm near.

You are intelligent, with a spectacular sense of humor. You love the past as much as I do. You love to cook and you love to eat. You share my passion for the perfect cappuccino, for the first fiddlehead ferns in April, for a glass of steaming apple cider on a crisp October night. You wear a delicate floral perfume—not too much, perhaps only a suggestion of scent, but it has a language all its own, for me. You are not, thank God, one of those bony clotheshanger types; you have an exquisite figure that could only be described as lush, and at night, your body is my personal map of the universe.

I want you because you are clearly the most interesting woman in the room. I also want you because every other man wants you as well, even though I would never admit this in a million years, even to myself. You are an eagle who needs shelter from the storm, an elegant woman who likes to curl up in bed and listen to the rain, a gourmet cook who understands the importance of cookies and milk on a bad day. You are as powerful and gentle and contradictory as I am, and once I find you I will court you for the rest of our lives.

## HOW TO DRIVE ME WILD

Make it soft. Make it subtle. Imply rather than ask. Do not fall all over me. I hate that. And take your time. Patience is the secret of eroticism.

I'm looking for a signal from you. I won't begin until I see the surrender in your eyes. I will follow your mood, because I can, like no other male in the universe. I can read you, and I will wait for the moment between us to be right.

So let us follow each other. Resist me, just the tiniest, tiniest bit. Oh, go ahead. Just enough until I'm unconditionally hooked, until I'm following you, until our thoughts and our signals are dancing back and forth and I can feel your longing for me. I love your cool, controlled look, with that suggestion of the wild, polite, unknowing young girl. I love the music you've chosen; they played it the night we met, didn't they? And how marvelous to have candles—two dozen? I hope you got them on sale—all over the house.

Now take off your blouse. Slowly. You put the barest flicker of perfume in your bra, didn't you? No, go more slowly than that! You're not used to being savored, are you? I may have to teach you. Good.

Now kiss me. Kiss my eyes and my face and the insides of my hands and the tips of my fingers and tips of other things. Tell me what you think of me in your kisses; let them be a secret language. I love the way you move—you are so sensual I can barely contain myself.

Now tell me a secret: you're not used to coming with a man inside you, are you? And you thought I didn't know that. I'm going to slowly, slowly take

off your clothes, and I want you to tell me all about
it. And I'm going to slowly, slowly take you. So
slowly that you won't know it's happening at first.
I need to take you in a way you've never dreamed
of being taken.

Lie back and look at me. Never take your eyes
from me. Don't move. That's my job. Don't move
for as long as you can stand it. There. Do you like
what I'm doing? Tell me. Show me. Let me hear
your pleasure.

## CONFIDENTIALLY YOURS

### * What He Won't Tell You

The Crab would like you to do 90 percent of the
seduction work, so he can feel sure of his welcome,
before he makes his move. See, if you seduce him
first, you can't possibly reject him later, right? And
if anything goes wrong, it can't be his fault, because
you started it.

Get it? Good. Mr. Crab likes to feel as safe as
possible at all times. This has its upside. When he
finally invites you to dinner, there will be Mozart,
five dozen candles, a fifteen-course meal, and a bottle of Cristalle Rose on ice. The Crab leaves nothing
to chance.

On the other hand, have you noticed the holes in
his clammy, crummy old sweater? The moth-eaten
hat? The Crab dresses for contentment, and the
Crab is thrifty. He sees no economic or emotional
reason to throw out his favorite, thirty-year-old fly-
fishing hat, or the boots he inherited from Dad—
why, all they need is little polish and they'll be
good for another fifty years. Waste not, want not.

Does the Crab really cling? What are claws for?

Some women like being clutched around the ankles as they leave for work in the morning—it makes them feel needed. If you've never experienced the Crab Death Grip, you've probably never tried to get away from him for a breath of fresh air. Alone.

The astrological symbol for Cancer is 69. This is appropriate. Sex, to Cancer, is something he can put in his mouth. As children, Cancers suck their thumbs far before the usual age, and this progresses to breast sucking and hours of oral sex. The only problem he has is knowing when to stop. You may have to fling him out of bed with your feet, screaming "Enough! Enough! I can't take anymore!" If you have a strange part of your body that needs licking, turn it in his direction. Look parched and withered. He'll know what to do. If he's in a bad mood, however, expect a long dry spell. Make love? He can barely make it out of bed.

## ✳ The Bad Stuff

Is he hypersensitive? Nah. But have all the mirrors in your house specially altered so he looks tall and slender whenever he sees himself. The Crab makes compliments a real challenge. If you remark that he looks ruggedly handsome tonight, he concludes that he must have looked frail and repulsive this morning. Oh, why didn't you tell him the painful truth? Was there a hidden message in that statement?

Answer this question carefully, or you will launch an episode of sulking, an activity at which the Crab is a black belt master. There is Sulking as a Postmodern Art Form, Sulking as Precognitive Therapy, the Sulking Mind Control Method, the Death Ray Sulk, the New Age Sulk (with crystals), the Kamikazi Sulk (he's going down and he's taking you with him), the special Mother's Day Sulk (she wasn't there for him), the Pet Hamster Sulk (he never had one), Sulking for Fun and Profit, and Aerobic Sulking for the Nineties.

You've heard that Cancer suffers from secret feelings of inadequacy? Beware the afflicted-victim act that your tender Crab will try and foist upon you! Mr. Crab is about as victimized as Clark Kent in a tiny phone booth—a petty annoyance, but nothing Mr. Kent can't handle. You will come to realize that your modest, retiring Crab is quietly running your life, as well as the lives of your family, guests, and pets, all the while protesting bravely about the lack of understanding and empathy he's experiencing.

Furthermore, remember that whatever it is, It's Not The Crab's Fault. Write down these words and paste them to your makeup mirror. It is not his fault and he couldn't help it, he didn't do it, they made him, it wasn't fair, he had no choice, how could you—my God, when he was breaking his back for you—how could you even suggest— where is your devotion?—you're not suggesting he had any *choice* in the matter, you're not—you're not accusing him of being wrong!! You're not blaming him—spotless, cherished, dear little him, or suggesting that he was culpable in any way for what happened, are you? This isn't, no, it couldn't be— a criticism!! You couldn't be suggesting that he has deficiencies, or shortcomings that would make him do such a thing of his own free will!!!! Surely not!!! He thought that you said you loved him!!! *Well, prove it!* Or he will hold his breath until he turns blue and *then you'll be sorry!*

The Crab is the soul of discretion. This means you won't be able to pry any deeply personal information out of him, such as his phone number, his address, his height, his weight (never), how he feels about you, how much he makes (hah!), whether or not he's mad, and where he's taking you tonight. The upside of this is that you will become an expert in the ancient Chinese art of face reading, since the Crab prefers that you intuit what he is thinking and feeling at all times. Don't you love him? He thought so. So if you would just read his mind from now on and spare him the agony of having to SAY what he wants, life would be infinitely improved.

## ✳ How Cancer Likes His Women

Crabs have been known to fall hopelessly in love with darkly beautiful, romantic neurotics, whom they try to nurture and save. However, when it comes to marriage, the Crabman tends to choose a well-functioning achiever—she who can hold her own in intelligent discussions, who can wield a balance sheet or a sauté pan with witty flair, and who always looks serenely, elegantly, sensual. Even in blue jeans, with no makeup, over a campfire. (Not that the Crab would be caught dead near a campfire. To the Crab, roughing it means trimming the petunias.)

Warning: the Crab is a superb blend of feminine intuition and masculine achievement. Not only does he know that you'd secretly love to go to Paris, he can probably afford to take you there. If not now, then soon. He also loves being in love and is a master of romance. What this means is: he is incredibly easy to fall in love with. And he's not so easy to fall *out* of love with (remember the Death Grip), so don't get entangled unless you're serious.

The flip side of Crab romance is Crab codependence.

## * What The Crab Sees When He Looks At You

You are an elegant earth goddess disguised as an modern, witty woman. You body suggests rolling, dark nights of indescribable pleasure, of which you are somehow modestly unaware in the light of day. You laugh easily and often. Mr. Crab likes a strongly defined physical type: dark, sensuous, and exotic or blond, healthy, and Nordic—whatever your looks, you will be a standout.

The Crab is definitely the marrying kind, and he makes a fabulous, if demanding, husband. He not only wants his own personal domestic goddess, he wants a graceful, cultivated companion that he can proudly escort to business and pleasure functions. You can whip up a perfect Caesar salad while quoting from *Archeology* magazine and chilling the Chablis to just the right temperature. Furthermore, you have this fascinating (to a Crab) hint of the little girl about you—a well-bred, shy, sexy little girl, who drops her inhibitions along with her clothes when he manages to get you alone.

## * What Turns Him On

Don't play games. Don't come on strong, and don't be vulgar. The Crab wants a lady, the kind from the era when that term really meant something. In fact, the past is one of his favorite places to be, so any suggestion of yesteryear will go far toward warming his heart. What turns him on is beauty and wit. If you are not witty, listen to him raptly, since he undoubtedly is. He will find you extremely clever.

Pay close, enormously sympathetic attention to his complaints, of which there will be an over-abundance. Do not pry into his affairs—i.e., don't ask him his last name until he offers it to you. But do give him a few secrets to unravel. The Crab will burst a blood vessel before he will let a suspected secret get away.

## ✶ What Rules The Crab

Security. The Crab can never be too safe. What safety requires of him depends upon his particular idiosyncrasies: securities, stocks, compound interest, an umbrella policy, electronic surveillance, a large guard dog, close friends, a cozy spouse, a snug family, an unleaky roof, fleece-lined boots, all of the above.

# THE CHASE

## ✶ His Secret Paradox

He is shy, self-effacing, and courteous. A harsh spotlight would melt a typical Cancer quicker than snow in July, unless he has Leo somewhere prominently in his chart. But the shy, endearing little Crab needs to mastermind everything that's going on—quietly, shyly, and endearingly. Sort of like the tiny sandcrab who controls the wind and the tides. Impossible? Cancer is one of the four cardinal signs of leadership. So if you think you're running the show, think again.

## ✶ How To Bewitch Cancer

Be flirtatious, but don't make direct suggestions—let him do that. Be very, very friendly, and send him "Yes, please" signals with just a soupçon of sexiness. You also have a modest touch of resistance—just a hint. Cancer loves this type of infinitely subtle dance. You've heard the phrase "A boy chases a girl, until she catches him"? If you want a Cancer man, this is your motto. So while you are simultaneously encouraging him, back off, just a bit, and you'll get him to follow you. It's a marvelous tango, and it's just what he loves.

P.S.—Do you have a sore throat? Wear your most fetching Irish lace bed jacket and allow him to come over with tea and honey. He will arrive with a portable medicine chest. The Crab adores making a fuss over you almost as much as he adores having a fuss made over him. So let him! Your turn to play nurse will come, never fear.

## ✳ Don't . . .

Criticize. Do not even remember how to criticize. Do not even associate with people who remember how to criticize. Tell him you thought hypochondria was a female disease. Ask what he's thinking—before, during, or after sex. Tell him you always defend his spending habits to your friends. Clean out his drawers. While he's sulking to get your attention, hand him some Alka-Seltzer. Serve sugar-free, fat-free, gluten-free food. Buy him a talking scale for his birthday. Drink cheap wine.

## ✳ Who He Likes To Bed

The angels created this man for romance. But in the absence of true love, he will bravely make do with flings—serial, monogamous flings, however. The Crab is not into full-scale debauchery. To entice him: be beautiful, be witty, and have very good manners. Be elegant, be amusing, be soft. Laugh at his crazy humor, analyze the béchamel sauce with him, and choose Clos de Vougeot for supper. All important: give him the signal that he can move in. He likes to swoop down and conquer, but only after he's assured of victory.

## ✳ Who He Likes To Wed

Mom. And why not! When they made her, they broke the mold. Bear in mind that Cancer males either worship their mothers or are desperately estranged from them—it amounts to the same thing. So you will either be living up to Mother or surpassing her, depending on his needs.

Try to imagine his mother as a wonderful, interesting woman. This way you will not grind your teeth when he tells you that your birthday and Mom's birthday are—wow!—two days apart. Or that your chicken fricassee is actually better than hers (like you care). Or that your strong-minded complexity doesn't threaten him because that's what he experienced as a child, etc., etc., etc.

## ✳ What He's Secretly Afraid Of

How long do we have?? He's a dull-and-duller lover and his weenie is too teeny. That nasty waiter used regular pepper on his Caesar salad. The sea level is rising and his poor little house will be under water by 2008. Women prefer the Marlboro Man. His parakeet snarled at him this morning— it's an omen. He has such a nice, *round*, face. Yes, money can buy love, and he'll never know the difference. He looks like the Pillsbury Doughboy in a tuxedo. No one will ever understand his need to feel safe. Everyone will understand his need to feel safe and they will laugh hysterically. Perhaps he's oversensitive.

## * When To Say Yes

When you say yes to an impassioned Crab, it will be unforgettable. He will court you beautifully, relentlessly, and he will take all the time in the world. And when the moment comes, there will be moonlight, and expensive champagne, and the flowers you told him you liked one day long ago. When to say yes? You will know. Because he will know, because he has waited until the mood is right, until you are both ready, until you are both mad with longing for each other.

# THE COUP DE GRACE

## * His Sexual Secrets And Desires

How to send him into orbit: mix food with sex in any way possible. Cancer men like to talk and laugh in bed. However, they are easily wounded—never point and laugh, or you may scar him for life.

Crabs love music, so let there be marvelous, moving, sensuous music. Invite him to a private picnic, on the floor of your living room. Crabs appreciate the finer things in life, so have a white linen picnic cloth, candles, and silver candlesticks. While you hand him an Austrian crystal glass of Perrier Jouet, lean over so that he can see the lacy top of the pale silk teddy you're wearing, teddies being another Cancerian proclivity. Let there be not dinner, but unforgettable edibles, such as toast points with caviar, chocolate-dipped strawberries, and a jar of honey.

Ask him if he would like a twilight massage. Take off your blouse, very, very slowly. Tell him to close his eyes, and softly, very softly, and slowly, very slowly, place your lips just next to his face. Do not actually touch his skin. Kiss him, but let your mouth touch his body only at the last possible second, and then only so he can barely feel it. Continue to do this along his face, his hair, and down his neck. Don't forget the ears.

Ask him if you can take off his shirt. Offer to remove something of yours so he will feel more comfortable. When he is half naked, continue with your massage, going very slowly, never actually touching his skin until the last possible moment, and then so lightly that your touch is the barest whisper. Take as long as you like. Cancerian men have extremely sensitive nipples. If they've never been kissed before, see if you can awaken them.

Continue to travel down his body. By this time, you are both completely naked. Move your lips all around his penis, but don't touch it. Take a long time. When he is off into orbit, take a small bit of butter from your picnic basket, and smooth it up and down his penis with your fingers. Make him glisten.

Then slowly reach for the jar of clover-flavored honey. Dip your fingers into it and spill some, just a little. Laugh. Tell him you're clumsy and you don't know where to wipe your hands. Then slowly, unconsciously spread the honey on the part of you he'd most like to taste, while you stare at him and smile. Laugh as you lick your fingers. Tell him it feels sticky, and ask him if he can do anything about it. When he says yes, gently position yourself over his waiting mouth, facing his penis.

Begin to lick all the butter off. Take your time. He should be occupied elsewhere.

Now, to completely enrapture this man, give yourself over to him, more and more and more until you can't remember where or who you are. Let go; let him take you to places you never dreamed about. Let go. Let the sounds of ecstasy escape from your lips and let your body shudder with pleasure. Let everything go—into him, his lips, his warm, waiting mouth, and the night.

### ✷ Shhh . . .

Sometime when he thinks he's seen it all, take one of your well-buttered fingers and gently massage his ass, around and around and around. When he stops tensing up, slide your finger inside. Do not move. Let it rest there. Move your finger once, only, about every minute and a half. Do this while you're bringing him to orgasm orally. And when he comes, slide out your finger, slowly, so that he feels it every inch of the way.

## AFTERGLOW: WHAT YOU NEED TO KNOW

### ✷ What Cancer Likes Better Than Sex

Security. And Cancer spells that word m-o-n-e-y. No, he does not love money for its own sake. He loves it for the walls and towers of safety that it can enclose him in, that perhaps may take away his deep-seated existential anxiety. (It won't, but it can buy him a reasonable facsimile.)

### ✷ Will He Marry His Best Lover Or Best Friend?

The Crab's standards for ideal womanhood exceed Homer's description of Helen of Troy. He is extremely picky; he can go for years without a deep sexual attraction, waiting patiently until *she* comes along. So the only answer to this is that Mr. Crab wants it all: a deep, deep friendship with a highly sensuous woman who adores sex. And he will keep going until he gets it right.

## ✳ What He Wants From You

Sympathy! Commiseration! Empathy! Compassion! Approval! Tune up that violin and be prepared to play for him at a moment's notice.

## ✳ What He Needs From You

Eternal certainty. That he is loved, that he is The One, that there is no one else in all the world like him, to you, ever, ever, ever, nor will there be, unto all eternity, and beyond, including all known and unknown universes, black holes, and planetary time warps.

## ✳ What He Won't Give Up For You

His nest egg. His various physical and mental safety nets. His antique silverware. Interestingly enough, for all his emotional clinginess, the Crab can be quite clear-eyed about a romance that's going nowhere. He may be desperately unhappy, he may cleave and clutch for a while, but he is too canny to slide into suicidal depression, bankruptcy, or disposition of his assets over a romance gone sour.

## ✳ What He Will Give Up For You

Um, a few of his more exotic worries, maybe. But mostly he will bring them all into the relationship, along with his teddy bear, his fish poacher, and his stamp collection.

## * How To Make Him Fall In Love With You, Really

His feelings can be so self-involved and so intense that he has trouble separating his daydreams from reality. If you're not careful, you'll exhaust yourself trying to live up to some romantic ideal that exists only in his overheated brain. Gently teach him that reality is not only safer than dreams; it is far lovelier.

The Crab needs a bit of easing into reality, however. It may take him time to belive that you are a lustful creature, for example; that you are a real woman with real needs and that you will quarrel with him occasionally. But these are all things that will actually make him more secure once he's grasped the concept. And while you are not perfect, he will realize how lucky he is that you are absolutely perfect for him, which is all he needs.

## * Make It Forever

Make sure he knows that you need privacy as well, and that you were not put on earth to coax him out of his moods. You want a relationship of enormous mutual sympathy, not a vortex of codependence. The Crab is an interesting reciprocal lover. He needs a woman who needs his beautiful emotional nurturing, yet who is strong and solid enough to nurture him right back.

While he is a magnificent protector and provider, he has weird insecurities, and he needs your rock-solid assurance that all is well. In time, he will feel so secure with you that he will not have to have his mind read in order to communicate. Share with

him always how much you love your home, your
garden, your kitchen, and your bed. And most of
all, let there be food, let there be sympathy, and let
there be love.

## CRUCIAL MINUTIAE

### ✳ What To Feed Cancer

Absolutely superb food. Marinate the tomatoes in
olive oil and herbs, and bake them in a slow oven.
Use good rosemary bread, and mash the imported
goat cheese with fresh thyme and rosemary. Layer
organically grown watercress as you slowly fold
the tomato–goat cheese sandwich together, and
saute it lightly for minute or two. Serve with chilled
Riesling, for a highly unusual flavor.

Offer him taste sensations even he didn't know
about: Château d'Yquem '69 with warmed fois
gras, Saint-Estèphe '64 with homemade focaccia
pizza.

Psst! As a child, did he dip Oreos in milk until
they were squishy? Did he favor peanut butter and
Fritos sandwiches? By all means ferret out these little gems—there will be quite a few—and serve
them to him on a rainy day when he's feeling blue.
Watch what happens.

### ✳ How To Take Care Of Your Crab

Cancer lives by the phrase "mind over body." He
was doing fine until that mood overtook him, all
because the UPS man seemed a trifle mean today.
Why did he say, "Sign here" in that tone of voice?
Why couldn't he have said, "Please sign here, sir,

and have a nice day"? Perhaps the Crab should have invited him in for coffee?

By now the Crab has a full-blown case of sniffles, as well as a sore throat, an iffy stomach—even his feet hurt. Red Alert!! Nothing less than world-class care will do!! Get out your best handwoven blankets. Gently put him to bed and rub menthol on his chest. Cover it with soft flannel. Take his temp and place a cool washcloth on his forehead. Spoon homemade chicken soup into his quivering mouth; plump the down pillows around his poor little face. You think this is overdoing it? You have not yet begun to fuss!

## ✳ For His Birthday

Give him fabulous collectibles—a fine old silver inkwell, a perfect small blown-glass vase. Cancer enjoys exquisite possessions, especially if he can pass them on to his great-grandchildren. He will undoubtedly have a collection—stamps, drinking cups, tiny silver snuffboxes—that you can add to. Unlike Leo, something larger-than-life is unnecessary. Small-and-exquisite will do just fine.

Kitchen gifts are always welcome, since many Cancer men are fantastic cooks who can turn out a good *pâte frisé* with their eyes closed. Or find a wonderful, old-fashioned restaurant from a bygone age, perhaps French or Victorian, and surprise him. Make sure it's gracious and harks back to a quieter, more serene era (the one he secretly wishes he lived in). He will be overjoyed at this attention to his palate, his imagination, and his thirst for romance—all in one quietly elegant package. And he will be amazed at your understanding of his most secret self.

◯ ☾ ● ☽ ◗

*Pat adelfi*
*7-24-63*

# leo

*Joe DeBasio*
*8-18-90*

### JULY 24 · AUGUST 23

## BEST LOVE MATCHES

Leo & Aries
Leo & Gemini
Leo & Libra
Leo & Sagittarius

He's standing in the center of the room, where he can talk to all the pretty women at once. He's charismatic, he's dominating, and he has a brilliant smile. He loves a challenge. He's Leo, the Lion.

## FAMOUS LEOS

Bill Clinton, Robert De Niro, Dustin Hoffman, Matt LeBlanc, Matthew Perry, Laurence Fishburne, Patrick Swayze, Sean Penn, Michael Douglas, Arnold Schwarzenegger, Magic Johnson, Christian Slater, Woody Harrelson, Wesley Snipes

## I AM

Rhett Butler, my dear, and I am looking hard for my Scarlett. Scarlett was a devil with the face of a Botticelli, and only one man alive could carry her up those stairs and make her sing about it the morning after.

But unlike Rhett, I do give a damn. Now and always. So don't be taken in by my soft-spoken, laid-back '90s persona. It's an act. There are worlds to conquer, and there is you, and I haven't got a lot of time.

You look confused! Spend an hour with me and a bottle of Dom and I'll tell you what you should do with your life. It's a gift I have. You think I'm bluffing? Come on! What's an hour? Look what Henry Higgins achieved with Eliza Doolittle. The woman was magnificent when he was finished with her. Trust me. By the way, you have beautiful hair; you should wear it just an inch shorter to show off your cheekbones. I'm right, aren't I? That's the hell of it, my dear, I'm always right. Give in now and avoid those tedious temper tantrums.

This party could use some class. I explained to the host that he shouldn't have served punch—how Dickensian. Punch is for kids at Christmas—not very sophisticated kids. I have an excellent case of single malt I could have sent over, if only I'd been consulted. And three dozen bottles of Veuve Clicquot. And what is this chip-and-dip scene? He must have hired Betty Crocker. I told him to let me know next time and I'll send over my personal caterer.

I can have any woman in this room. Want to bet? I'll bet you a diamond tennis bracelet against your virtue. No? You might win. But frankly, other women are fading from view tonight, ever since I laid eyes on you. I've been watching you for a while now. You look like you can't be tamed, and that brings a slow, lazy smile to my face. I had no idea you were with our host, but petty details never throw me.

You think I'm arrogant. The big secret, Pretty Eyes, is that it's all true. I really can master you in all your wild, stubborn, exciting self. I really can make you famished for it, and then I can make you beg for more. But you'll never hear any of this when we meet. I'm a brilliant strategist, so you'll never know what direction I'm coming from. And things happen on my time, no one else's, so you'll never know what's coming. It's impossible. Give in. Save all that *Sturm und Drang* for your mother. . . . Of course, if you were easy, I wouldn't want you, would I . . . ? See how difficult it is?

Life is a glorious kingdom, and I see myself as the ruler. Someday I will own the company I work for, and someday soon everyone will know who I am. I have to be the boss! Those who know how to rule should get on with it. That's why God created kings. You have the most darling lopsided grin. You look like you're three years old when you smile like that. You're pretending not to be interested. Fine by me, because I know you are. Besides, I love a virtuous woman.

What do I want out of life? I want the world at my feet and the stars at my beck and call. I want fame, fortune, glory, health, joy, rapture, and you. Humility? Humility is for saints—that's their job. And modesty is for virgins. I was never a virgin. I had impure thoughts when I was four, and I've never turned back.

I am strong—stronger than anyone you will ever meet, because my strength is not stubbornness; it comes from the heart. And try to control me—I love it. Go ahead! I love to watch a beautiful woman butt her head against a brick wall. It turns me on. You're so adorable when you lose. And it makes me want to smother you in roses and whisk you off to the Ritz for a nightcap.

Without vision, the people perish. Check it out, beautiful; it's in the Bible. And I'm here to give vision a face and a name. I need to be loved—first, last, and always—although I would never admit this under torture. My success isn't real until I see it right there in your eyes and in your heart.

## YOU ARE

My queen, my consort, my audience, my love. You are spellbinding. When I take you out for a small, exquisite dinner, you make every man in the room put down his fork just by the way you enter the room. This gives me soul satisfaction. You are not shrill, ostentatious or vulgar in anyway. You are grace personified; you move as if you've had dancing lessons since you were three. You are as arrogant as I am about all the right things: literature, music, art, wine, and what other people should do with their lives.

You are so stubborn that you're part mule. You think you know the way out of the forest, but you don't know the way out the door. And I don't care how high your IQ is. There's a hopelessly adorable part of you that needs tender loving care, and no other man can dominate you enough to accept it. You need me. Admit it! You'll never admit it until after the honeymoon, but you need me, my love, in ways you can't even begin to know.

You're independent, you're in control, you're

fast, funny, and furious, and you think of marriage as the death of your gloriously sovereign self. But the truth is, dear heart, it's the birth of a self you can only imagine. Only one man alive can give you the keys to this kingdom, and you just laid eyes on him. Oh, you'll fight me to the death, but I wouldn't have it any other way.

You are sheer, living, breathing excitement. The way you boil an egg is different from any other woman alive. You never, ever, bore me, and that makes you the eighth wonder of the world. Your witty, intelligent, sophisticated, challenging, stubborn little self is utterly precious to me. You are ravishing, unconquerable, and you are *mine*. Unutterably and irrevocably mine to love and to keep for the rest of our lives.

Now I just need to stick around until you wake up to the idea . . . I never get lost, so don't even think about it.

## HOW TO DRIVE ME WILD

That's it, go on and challenge me. Start an argument. You think you're in control; you think you know the score. My exquisite darling, you don't have a clue! I set this whole scene up before we met. I know what's going to happen, the only question is when.

I love an impossible woman. You're so aloof you drive me insane. But don't tease. Seduction acts make me yawn. I want you. I want your huge, shy heart and your wild, savage soul. I want to make love to them until dawn and then I want them beside me forever.

By the way, I appreciate the king-size bed (nice touch) and the silk sheets, and that's a real fire, isn't it? And you've kept the rose I gave you and hidden it beneath your pillow. And there's the little bag of peanuts we didn't eat at the ball game. You are moving me deeply. Affection and sex are meant to go together; I was hoping you knew that. . . .

But how many mirrors do you have? Five? Barely enough! Stand in front of them and take off your clothes. Unbutton that blouse, one button at a time. Tell me what you want me to do to you. Slowly. Slip the blouse off your shoulders. Turn so I can see the slope of your breasts in the mirror. I appreciate the candles. Hand-dipped, aren't they? You look magnificent in this light. Face me and take off your skirt. There. I love watching you all gleaming and naked.

Slowly reach for that jasmine oil. Rub your breasts with it. Grasp your nipples and make them hard. That's it. Now let your hand wander downwards. Touch yourself. Don't take your eyes off me. Open your mouth. Let me watch your breathing. Tell me what you're thinking, softly. I want to hear you. Now. Louder. I want to watch you explode. And then I want you to take your fingers and let me lick them, as I tie your hands behind your back. I love watching you yield to me like this.

You want me to touch you, but you have to ask for it. Kneel on the bed. Face me and show yourself to me, all wet and glistening for me. I'll satisfy you, darling, but not yet. First I want you to kneel down. Let me see your breasts hanging like pale pink flowers over my penis. Lift your ass so I can watch it in the mirror. Ask me if you can take me in your mouth. Ask me. Tell me you want it. Tell me what you'd like to do to me. Now kiss me, up and down. I know it's awkward with your hands tied. I love that. Use your tongue. Slowly! You will never make

me come, dear; I alone control my timing. Go
slowly. Make it slippery and wet. I'll wait, barely,
until I can no longer stand it, and then I'll lift you
onto me so I can watch your face and your breasts
when I come inside.

You never thought you could come in this position, did you? You never thought you'd like being
tied up. You never thought a lot of things, and your
surprise is bewitching me til I'm insane with desire.
I want you beside me always—tonight as well as
tomorrow morning, and all the mornings after.

## CONFIDENTIALLY YOURS

### ✶ What He Won't Tell You

He is not a snob. Only aspiring peasants are snobs.
He is the standard by which snobbism defines itself. You see the difference.

You've heard of "The Princess and the Pea"?
Well, meet the Prince and the Pea, he who per-
ceives the hard, annoying nub of legume through
twenty mattresses and cannot sleep for the pain.
His Highness is a tad sensitive. If he doesn't wear
silk underwear, he will soon. Cotton is so coarse
next to his skin—why, he gets a rash just thinking
of what his epidermis has to endure. And handwoven linen sheets are a necessity! His Majesty gets
insomnia from polyester.

The Lion has extraordinary patience with details—in his next life, when he's a Virgo. In
this one, however, details are for the palace guard,
and who is he to worry about phone numbers and
gas bills when he is planning victory campaigns
and running everyone's grateful little lives for
them?

Ah yes, pride. Pride is not one of the seven deadly sins; according to the Lion, it is one of the seven deadly virtues. And that is where he leaves it—to the dead. The living, breathing king of the jungle is not proud! He is sublime! There are peons who would refer to him as arrogant, conceited, haughty, and smug. These peons are but crabgrass in the great Serengeti of life. True, he has more gifts, glory, and splendor than others. But His Magnanimousness cannot wait to share them with you, his loving vassal.

In the Middle Ages, it was the King's privilege to sleep with any bride in the kingdom on her wedding night. This hideous practice was called *droit du seigneur*. Much the same idea applies here. The Lion can flirt his face off with every woman at the party, my dear—but you cannot. You may quote Betty Friedan until you are purple, to no avail. He may ogle, banter, and tease, but should you sigh too loudly at a Daniel Day-Lewis movie, His Highness will gently remind you that you didn't enjoy it that much. Agree. If you want him to stick around.

## ✱ The Bad Stuff

Has the King made a mistake? Did he forget to call you last night? Somehow, this is your fault. You failed to indicate that he should use a telephone. Perhaps you meant fax. Perhaps you meant carrier pigeon. How was he to follow incomplete guidelines such as these??

Besides, you did not adequately convey your desperate need for this call. Perhaps it was only a vague whim on your part. A wistful notion. How, he asks the gods above, is he supposed to respond

o such flimsy, diaphanous themes? And now! Gad!
Now you have the gall—the unmitigated gall!!—to
reproach him for this miserable, petty sin of omis-
sion! When he was busy mapping out your future
for you! *This is the thanks he gets!! Is there no one in
the universe who can appreciate his grandeur of vision??
His greatness of soul?? Without this incessant paltry,
petty, cheap, miserly, insufferable nit-picking??*

Now is your chance! Shyly admit that you mis-
spoke yourself, and apologize for your pitifully
inadequate communiqué. Then he can magnificently, affectionately forgive you. This constitutes
the sum total of the Royal Apology. Analyze this
technique. You will need it.

Him, dramatic? Oh, the indignity of such a question! Dah-*ramma*?????? Oh, he could bleed from the
teeny pores of his delicate skin over such a despi-
cable lie! Wounded, he will flee—No! He never
flees!!—wounded, he will stalk off to a lair in the
misty treetops—No! He hates mist!!—wounded, he
will stalk off to a secret forest den, there to seethe
over the sheer insignificance of those cretins with
whom he is forced to mingle his royal self.

There are techniques on How to Have an Orgasm
Privately Without Disturbing Your Man's Pleasure.
Study up on them, because His Highness cannot be
bothered to study up on you. Sexually, that is.
What are concubines for? When the lights go down,
so do you, preferably to the floor. All the better to
service (oops!), serve him, my dear. When he
chooses to serve you, however, best your moans of
pleasure be loud enough to wake the dead, in gratitude for this visitation from the king.

Also, if deary is weary some evening and in need
of rest (a rare and remarkable event), you should
be grateful for his gracious provision of a health-

giving pause in the action. Should you be wear
and in need of rest, however, your abstinence wi
be viewed as mulish, uncharitable, miserly, and ;
black blot on the purity of the relationship. H
hopes this weariness will not be repeated.

He's not a bully, however, because real bullie;
aren't doing it for your own good. Furthermore
real bullies aren't devastatingly charming, and yo
never feel like thanking them for browbeating yo
into improving your life. Once you feel the effect;
of the Lion's influence on your humble existence
you will never again be tempted to use that nasty
word.

## ✷ How Leo Likes His Women

Irresistibly challenging. You do not come wher
you're called. Well, not the first five times. You are
an optimist with a heart too big to indulge in petty
criticisms, and all criticisms are petty to His Maj
esty. You have a literate, witty mind that does *no*
back down in an argument. You are generous anc
enjoy life at the top, which is where he intends for
both of you to reside. You live life in the fast lane—
even if only in your mind—and you have dozens
of fascinating passions which you gladly share with
him. If he can keep up with you.

## ✷ What The Lion Sees When He Looks At You

You have presence. Even if you are the shy, modes;
type, you have a shy, modest, unmistakable presence that makes people sit up and take notice. And
you have glamour. This man is nuts for glamour
He needs to show you off, to be extravagantly
proud of you at all times.

Furthermore, you are morally elegant. You do

not indulge in dirty jokes, at least not in public, at least not until you know each other very well. And not even then. Although you are not in the least vulgar, you have a suggestion of the geisha about you—independent though you are—that only he can see. And that only he can bring out.

## ✶ What Turns Him On

A challenge. The King is a restless workaholic who lives at warp speed—he has to, in order to cram in all those careers, love affairs, travels, art, and basketball games before he retreats to that big palace in the sky. But unlike Aries, who loves to be teased, Leo definitely does not. You must be witty, aloof, self-kept, generous, and alluring, and you must be utterly genuine about all of it.

## ✶ What Rules The Lion

Ruling you. And the rest of the known galaxy. The Lion takes his guardianship as a sacred trust—and he's good at it. Being a loyal subject isn't so bad, actually. Think of the presents! Leo is the King of Present-Givers. The more he takes beneficent care of others, the more power he gets. And Leo positively bastes himself in power.

## THE CHASE

## ✶ His Secret Paradox

His Majesty needs to rule your life, but he needs to be loved for himself alone. Louis XIV had the same problem. Leo, in fact, cannot truly reign without being loved. He responds to genuine, unconditional loving like no one else in the zodiac. The

more deeply he is loved, the more power he has to
make magic happen in your life together. Remember this when he is plotting to conquer new king-
doms. There is only one kingdom that really
matters to him—the kingdom of the heart.

## ∗ How To Bewitch Leo

This cat is a stalker. He loves to hunt—so pursue
your own path and let him track you, physically
and mentally, and let it be a huge, glorious challenge to him. After all, if you're easy prey, of what
use are his superb stalking skills? He knows he can
have any woman he wants. What if—gods
above!—what if he couldn't have . . . you? *Impossible!* Plant this teeny doubt in his mind, and he will
focus on you with petrifying intensity. You won't
see it, but your skin will prickle as he shadows you.
He's on the hunt. Meanwhile, flirt magnificently
with just the right touch of antagonism that makes
it all electrical and inspired.

## ∗ Don't . . .

Interrupt him. Do anything else, such as breathe,
while he's talking. Read aloud from *Kama Sutra for
Beginners.* Wait til he's made up his mind for you,
then make another suggestion. Forget to ask his advice. Tell dirty jokes in public. Tell him you went
bargain-hunting for his birthday. Rave about your
favorite rock star. Ask him where he was last night.
Yawn at the wrong moment (and every moment is
wrong). Dare to offer advice. Rain on his parade.

## ∗ Who He Likes To Bed

A highly sexual, challenging woman whom he can
reduce to a grateful, panting slave by the sheer

force of his erotic power. You are unconstrained, dynamic, and adventurous. You force him to pursue you. And, most important, you have a life. His Majesty hates wallflowers. Invite him skiing—oh, hasn't he skied before? Tsk. By the time you reach the mountain, Leo will have secretly rented a dozen Olympic ski tapes and hired an expert to teach him the finer points. You cannot take this man by surprise, but you can spend your life trying, and he will adore you for it.

## ✴ Who He Likes To Wed

*Mon Dieu!* His Queen, of course! Who else is worthy? She who can reflect his power, majesty, and glory, because she has enough of her own.

The King wants it all: an independent, elegant woman who will cater to him, and only him, for the sheer joy of it. A superwoman who doesn't mind serving him (sometimes). He doesn't want to break your will, he just wants it to bend occasionally, for his pleasure. You see the distinction.

Her Majesty should also have strength of character, so that Mr. King can relax occasionally, when he's off-duty, and expose the gentler, softer side of himself. Furthermore, she should be autonomous enough to challenge him constantly, so that he is never bored. And last, she must make him feel loved and needed like no one else on earth.

## ✴ What He's Secretly Afraid Of

That boredom builds character. Napoleon needed growth hormones. Deep down, no dictator is benevolent. Flirting makes your hair fall out. He will have to work for someone else for the rest of his life. Was that a stifled yawn he just observed? Did

he really achieve all this, or did he just wave
wand and have it all appear? Will it all disappea
someday when he's not looking?

## * When To Say Yes

Timing! Timing! Don't disappoint this Master o
Romance by either giving in too early or prolong
ing things for too long. It's tricky. When you are
looking out over the moss-covered cliff, beneath the
golden harvest moon, with the wind silvering al
the trees and you feel his eyes staring down into
your soul, *Now!!! This is it!!! Now!!!*

## THE COUP DE GRACE

### * His Sexual Secrets And Desires

The man is romance personified. He is also dra
matic, highly sensual, and sentimental, and he ap-
preciates class. Get out your best crysta
wineglasses. In fact, get out your best of everything
Leo will graciously approve. Have soft music in the
background. Let there be roses, and candlelight
and chilled Montrachet.

Stun him. Greet him at the door wearing a merry
widow that pushes your breasts up and out so the
nipples wink at him all night long. Wear your cor-
set, breast rouge, and nothing else—except 6-inch
heels. Ask him if he likes what you're wearing
Hint that you're not wearing panties. And you
promise not to cross your legs or close your mouth
all night, so that you are totally accessible to him
Tell him you're his mistress until dawn.

Invite him into the bedroom. (Your bed is old

oak, your carpet is plush, and your pillows are goose down. You have linen sheets. If they aren't, they look like they are.) Tell him you've waited all night to see him naked. Ask his permission to undress him. Slowly remove his shirt and his pants. Take off his underpants, slowly, with your teeth. (It can be done.)

When he is naked, ask if you can taste him. Give him a hand-held camcorder and ask if he'd like to film you while you go down on him. But first, ask him to tie your hands. Ask him how he'd like you positioned. Make sure you have plenty of mirrors in the room. As you bend over him, mention that you're imagining that there's someone—a man— watching from a corner of the room. Ask him if he can imagine someone taking you from behind while you suck him.

Now ask his permission to begin. Bend down and begin to kiss his penis. Tell him how huge it is. Thoroughly lick his balls and hold each one in your mouth, gently. By this time, he will be rigid with desire, and he will be giving you instructions, never fear. And every time he tells you what to do, say "Yes, Master" very softly. Take him in your mouth, and slowly move your head up and down, timing your movements to his rhythms. When he reaches his climax, keep your mouth there as you slowly savor and swallow him. (After all, he would do no less for you.) When he comes back to life, ask him if he would fulfill another fantasy. Hand him some silk scarves and ask him to tie you up. He will melt with ecstasy.

When you are both lying in blissful afterglow, tell him he is your Once and Future King. He will weep with joy. Inside.

## ∗ Shhh . . .

He loves quickies. In the car, in the shower, on the back porch, in the broom closet—ambush him, rip off his clothes, and make it hot and dirty. Do it just often enough so that he never knows what to expect.

# AFTERGLOW: WHAT YOU NEED TO KNOW

## ∗ What Leo Likes Better Than Sex

Power, as in "to govern." The Lion's secret desire is to rule the world—or, at the very least, his world. Remember that His Majesty is street-smart in a delightfully scary way. Don't second-guess his instincts, or you'll live to regret it.

## ∗ Will He Marry His Best Lover Or Best Friend?

His best lover, no question, who shares his deep interest/passion/obsession with sex, and who has—surprise!—become his dearest friend. After all, no one else can keep up with him.

## ∗ What He Wants From You

Worship. Idolization. Deification. The Lion wants radical god-status, and he does love to be served. If you don't cook, get take-out and serve it to him on your best china. Make sure there are two or three courses at dinner. Light candles in silver candlesticks. Hand him a warmed towel to refresh his hands and face. Rub his extremities with Tiger Balm (not the one in the middle).

### ✴ What He Needs From You

To know he is loved. Er, admired. He really is a great guy, and he urgently needs to see this when he looks in your eyes. Furthermore, he cannot function in peak form if he does not receive the proper esteem. A Lion who feels invisible is a miserable Lion. He needs you to mirror his finest qualities back to him, so that he can really believe they exist. If he has chosen you to do this, feel honored. Not just any peasant will do.

### ✴ What He Won't Give Up For You

The throne. His need to efficiently run everyone's life—including yours. His daring schemes for the future. His daily lectures on how to improve your life. His disdain for details. His need to flirt—flirting is like water to this man. His time-warp schedule.

### ✴ What He Will Give Up For You

Why this talk of abdication? A King does not abdicate! A King enfolds and encloses all lesser realities into his magnificent self.

Psst! However! When he feels well and truly loved by you, Leo will grandly sweep all lesser females out the palace door. You will be his only Queen and there will be no rivals, and he will proudly announce this to the world at every opportunity.

### ✴ How To Make Him Fall In Love With You, Really

Love him for who he really is before you get any of the gifts, attention, seductive behavior, or cozy advice. Love him so that it is clear that he is loved first and last for himself and not for his magnificence (they really are separate), and he will melt at your feet.

His Majesty is terribly vulnerable. He needs you to tell him how wonderful he is, and he really is wonderful. But if you tell him, it comes true for him deep down in his great, bursting heart. And then he will outperform the gods themselves and lay the universe at your feet.

P.S.—To keep a Leo eternally contented, make it abundantly clear that he reigns supreme in the boudoir. Wear your satisfaction on your sleeve. When you appear with him in public, look deeply satisfied. Snort pityingly at other, lesser men. (Hint: all men are other and lesser.) Are those violins sweetly playing? No, it's your Lion, purring more beautifully than Paganini.

## ✴ Make It Forever

You are a consort. You are not a subject or a slave. There are things you will not put up with. When you ask his advice, make it clear you are asking for friendly input, not a royal decree, and that you will be making up your own mind. This requires cunning, since the Lion actually wants and needs to be consulted on your every move.

Success sometimes puzzles the Lion. Perhaps he really thinks he did it all on charm. But if you're there to remind him that he did it on guts, brains, and brilliance, he will heave a deep sigh of relief and wrap you in his huge, warm arms. (Even if his arms aren't huge, they are inside.)

And last, love him with everything you have, and he will open his great, splendid, cavernous heart and love you back a thousandfold. It is magnificently possible to tame this beast, and he makes a superb husband. A beloved Lion—generous, wise, tender, passionate and faithful—is a wondrous sight to behold.

## CRUCIAL MINUTIAE

### ✱ What To Feed Leo

Compliments! Give him two or three per meal. As for mere food, the King has the simplest of tastes— he likes only the best. A special dinner? Let your table be set with French linen, Irish crystal, and English silver. Have calla lilies flown in from New Zealand. Forget mere steak and salad! Serve him filet mignon, topped with duxelles and wrapped in filo dough, with onion confit. Offer him tiny buds of raddichio, arugula, and mesclun, with grilled pepper strips, bathed in balsamic vinegar–walnut oil dressing. Crumble aged chevre on top. He will bask in gastronomic afterglow—and take you out for a stupendous dessert!

### ✱ How To Take Care Of Your Lion

The Lion lives at the speed of nuclear fission. He's hale and hearty, but he constantly flirts with burnout. Definitely drag him off to a private cabin in the woods for some peaceful hours with the birds, the bees, and you. Create tranquil down-time for him, during which he doesn't have to dazzle anyone and he can relax with some (imported, Dutch, expensive) hot chocolate, a good book, and you, curled up next to him where he can find you instantly.

The King's emotions govern his health, so take

good care of them. Do not drizzle weepy, cautious showers of worry all over his sunny joy in life. Remember that there never was a male more susceptible to sweet-talk than your Lion. He can be coaxed out of the sulks and into his usual charm with agreeably mellow words of praise, and reminders of just how exciting and joyous life really is.

## \* For His Birthday

Think *big*, *extravagant*, and *luxurious*. Spare no expense! He never does. Handmade silk sheets (monogrammed, of course) or an Austrian down quilt for his lair. Have a masseuse arrive at his door and give him an at-home cranial/fascial massage. Find his baby pictures and put them all in sterling silver frames around the living room. Give him a globe, one that lights up and twirls around and is set in a mahogany stand. It will feed his fantasies. Start him a collection of miniature knights, especially the beautifully painted ones. It will make him feel at home.

◯ ☾ ● ☽ ◗

# virgo

## AUGUST 24 - SEPTEMBER 23

### BEST LOVE MATCHES

Virgo & Taurus
Virgo & Cancer
Virgo & Capricorn

He's helpful, he's funny, and he's very smart. He'll freshen your drink while he cracks you up with astute observations. He's cool. He's collected. He's Virgo, the Virgin.

## FAMOUS VIRGOS

Richard Gere, River Phoenix, Cal Ripken, Billy Ray Cyrus, Karl Lagerfeld, Sean Connery, Hugh Grant, Keanu Reeves, Charlie Sheen

## I AM

Busy. It's extremely difficult to find time to talk when all these ashtrays need emptying. I cannot

109

believe people still smoke. I have an ionizer in every room of my house, and one in the car, for road pollution. I'll just take these drinks out to the kitchen. I don't see any caterers; I'm sure they could use some help. I detest loud, noisy gatherings, anyway, don't you? I've come to this party only for business reasons.

You can never have a real conversation at these things, and all this perfume gives me a headache. Why do women insist on drenching themselves in artificial odors? Are other men rendered helpless by a liquid chemical by-product? I prefer a woman to smell like she's spent a misty day in the woods. With me. Besides, an ounce of Joy costs as much as four dental visits, did you know that? And look at this dust! If they've hired a housekeeper, she must be writing a novel in her spare time. I'm afraid to eat this food. No onion dip is maroon by nature. Perhaps it's someone's biology experiment.

. . . You've observed I'm critical. I wouldn't say "critical" in the sense of "derogatory" or "faultfinding." Faultfinding connotes disparagement, and I never disparage with an intent to depreciate. I prefer the word "discriminating"—although I can be finicky about food. Do you know it takes two years to completely digest a maraschino cherry? I carry enzyme tablets with me in case I swallow one by mistake.

And I tend to analyze people. I apologize if this is hard on you. It's excruciating for me. It's difficult being right about everything; I'm exhausted most of the time. I have to take retreats from the world just to recover.

I have been accused of cross-indexing my sock drawer. I resent this. I have a deep, metaphysical love for order. I find a perfect file system to be a beautifully peaceful experience, in the same way that mathematics imposes a system of harmony on chaos. I don't ask you to understand. I doubt you meet many men for whom a balanced checkbook is an epiphany.

I hate telling people I was born in September. When they find out I'm a Virgo, everyone guides me to their filing cabinet. I suppose they think my vibrations will automatically tidy up their mess. Hah! Mess is as mess does. And by the way, I am not a "virgin" except in the most spiritual sense. I may be solitary by nature; I may dwell in the still waters of the mind where I find a singular kind of purity. But I find women infinitely attractive, witty, challenging, and very, very available.

I seek order the way others seek excitement. I prefer to function behind the scenes, where I can precisely monitor what's going on. I've been called a workaholic, but this is silly. I simply enjoy perfection, whether on the job or in the home. Furthermore, although I like money, I work for security, not wealth, and I do not believe in waste.

Romance is fun if I can come back at night to my cool, temperature-controlled, sound-proofed bedroom, with the lightly starched sheets, my clock radio that regulates random emf waves, my centrifugal ionizer, and my books. I am not really a monk, as some have snidely suggested, but am I interested in marriage? I doubt it. It's just so difficult to share one's privacy. I have places inside that no one will ever see; I need privacy like other men need air.

I dream sometimes of a woman whose very presence is quietude; who has a marvelous store of common sense, and yet who could teach me sensuality. I'm probably looking for my anima, a self-projection at best. But there I go again, analyzing it all away. Now I feel guilty. One should open oneself to the possible. One should; it's just that one can't. Oh, bother!

I have a quiet heart. When I love, I love with a depth that connects me and my beloved to the eternal love; there is a spiritual side to Eros that I need to fulfill. I am sure that if I fell in love, it would be forever. But I don't speak of these things. Unless . . . Are you really out there? Do you really exist?

## YOU ARE

There. That is what I love best about you. You are there when I am moody, when I can't talk about things, when I need to be alone—you are quietly, calmly there. Not to intrude, not to talk, even, but simply to let me know that I can return to you, when I'm ready. I cherish your calm, unruffled tranquility; you give me comfort of the soul, and that is so rare in this raucous, blaring minstrel-show of a world.

How do you achieve such a heavenly sensuality? I don't know, but I am humbly grateful for it. You have opened up whole new worlds for me at night, when we are private together, but you don't feel the need to talk about it. You have splendid common sense. You are the epitome of tact. You have the polished manners of a convent-bred schoolgirl. In fact, your educated mind is one of the things that draws me to you.

Your thank-you notes are written on mono-grammed, embossed, linen paper. You have a marvelous acuity for business. Whether you are a secretary or a CEO, you handle time and money with elegant ease. Speaking of money, you enjoy making it, saving it, and investing it. Thrift is a refined concept to you, not a dirty word.

The fact that you are a woman who could spend a long, sunlit afternoon at the museum pleases me enormously. You abhor emotional displays in any form. You are somewhat reserved, but how I love and understand that! And, last but never, never least, you are a magnificent listener. You are uniquely yourself, my dear, dear love, whom I love with a passion that I can never speak about.

## HOW TO DRIVE ME WILD

I am rather shy; I would prefer it, actually, if you would make the overture. Begin by moving slowly; I enjoy women who look like they dance when they walk. I appreciate the soft lights and the music in the background. I like the ambiance to be just right—well, I like the ambiance to be perfect. And this is just about perfect. Do you think you could turn down the lights just a tad? No, just a tad. That's it. Thanks. These glasses are lovely—they're so clean the light dances off them. And I like the chilled Chablis, so crisp and cool.

It is very peaceful here with you. Yes, I'd love a massage. I like the way your fingers work into my back. I like the delicately scented oil you're using; it's nongreasy, isn't it? I need something soothing like a massage to turn off the worry centers in my brain, so I can relax. By the way, you're doing a marvelous job. Where did you learn this technique? My jaw feels like it's melting. No, don't take off all my clothes . . . oh, go ahead. You're so slow, and so sensual. Don't stop.

How did you know I love having my buns

kneaded? I didn't know it myself until just now. I love the way you're stroking my cheeks, the way you're moving your fingers up the crack. Move your hand slowly, so slowly, down to the back of my balls. Massage them the way you're massaging my ass. With one hand on the small of my back and the other on my balls—where did you learn to do this? Now wrap me in one of those huge, soft towels.

I want you to undress so that you don't know I'm watching. Tell me you'll be right back. Move into the other room and let me see you undress by reflection, in the mirror. Slowly. So slowly. Don't look at me. I'll sip some Chablis. (I appreciate the ice bucket; it's still cold. I love thoughtful details like this.) I love that you don't cross the floor in the nude. I like the big, fluffy robe you've wrapped your naked body in. Watching you undress was an incredible turn-on. You've made me want you very badly.

Now turn me over and continue your massage. Let your robe fall open. Just slightly. Move your hands down my chest, down and around my penis, slowly, gently, both hands, gently. Let your robe fall open a little more. I can barely stand this. With one hand on my penis and one hand moving between my balls and my ass, your pace is exquisite. Come here; come on top of me. Let your robe fall open, please. Let me come inside you. Now. Yes. Yes. Perfect.

## CONFIDENTIALLY YOURS

### ✷ What He Won't Tell You

Mr. V is not into P.D.A.—public display of affection. A discreet hand-squeeze or a warm smile means "You are my cherished one, but I will not embarrass you by saying so in public." And you're not one of those women who wants a dozen tired roses and chemically altered, high-cholesterol chocolate on Valentine's Day, are you? He didn't think so. His love is too mystical and deep to be violated by tawdry commercialism. How fortunate that you feel the same way.

When you are with this man, never forget that Cleanliness is next to Godliness. One Virgo we know performed oral sex on his lover while she was lying on his new, clean, white couch. Five minutes afterward, when he thought she was in the bathroom, she caught him wiping off the sofa with Lysol. So don't worry if your Virgo starts washing dishes before you've had dessert, or eats with a dishtowel thrown over his shoulder, in case of spills. He's just being true to himself.

If Virgo's looking at you for marriage, he'll look and look and look and look. His greatest asset is that he sees things with scientific precision. His worst fault is that he sees things with scientific precision. You're under the Great Microscope of the Zodiac. But remain calm. His purpose is pure. Soon you will really start to enjoy the tingly feeling that Big Brother is watching. This is lucky, since you will be living that way for the rest of your life.

Mr. V may dream of a woman whose soul is quietude, but she'd better have a good job, a sound investment portfolio, and a solid grasp of inflationary spending. And make him look good in front of the boss. And be up on the latest critical reviews. And run a smooth, effortless household. And have a trim, fit figure. And be content with the quiet life. And be knowledgeable on the latest health breakthroughs. And be able to converse on a wide range

of topics. And . . . you see why he puts off marriage.

## ✳ The Bad Stuff

Do you like to lie abed in the morning, savoring
the sleepy touch of beloved flesh?

Not anymore you don't! From now on it's *Hup!
Ho! Afterglow!* Virgo is *up!* with the sun and *out!* on
the track, listening to Spanish language tapes on
the Walkman as he puts in his fifty laps. After that,
it's five hundred sit-ups as he watches his video
instruction course, "Great Philosophers of the
Western World, Part II."

Then hippity-hop to the kitchen, where his brew-
er's yeast has been simmering in pineapple juice,
along with a half-tablespoon of lecithin, a half-
teaspoon of kelp, and two packets of Nature's
Broom. And it's only six o'clock in the morning!
Heidy-ho to the bathroom where *oooopppps!* someone's been using his washcloth!! He never folds it
with two folds like that!! He hates to accuse any-
body, but putting his face in a washcloth that has
wiped someone else's face is unthinkably revolt-
ing!! Yech!! (Never mind where he put his face just
last night—that's different. Sort of.)

Virgo puts the fun in dysfunctional. He worries
for all us flippant souls who are not on twenty-
four-hour fret duty, so disturb him not in his lonely
vigil. And never seek to separate him from his anxiety—he is his anxiety, and let no man tear them
asunder. Instead, welcome to Zen and the Art of
Worrying.

Is Virgo into splitting hairs? He can make his
own paintbrush out of half a strand. But he would
say that he is critical in a discriminating—not de-

rogatory—sense. It pains him to tell you. But he swallows his pain and tells you anyway.

Cook him your best pasta dinner, for example, and watch what happens: "The spaghetti was in the water just thirty seconds too long, wouldn't you say, dear? Al dente pasta really requires meticulous commitment. This is more like chewing gum than pasta, sweetheart. And we were quite frisky with the oregano, weren't we? But what a noble effort, darling! You really should consider ground sirloin in the meatballs, though. You don't want them too rubbery. Of course, if they're cooked on low for nine hours instead of medium for two and a half, you won't have that problem. And this sprig of rosemary on top. Clever. Not very authentic, but clever. . . ."

At this point, you'll feel like stuffing him in the oven til he's good and done.

As if that weren't enough, Virgo is also vacation-challenged. He's a workaholic who can't leave the office until the computer has been sprayed with antiseptic. Getting him to relax is like getting the Rock of Gibraltar to melt and ooze into the Mediterranean. Maybe if you kidnapped him to a private resort that had a twenty-four-hour drugstore in the lobby, and hired a cranial/sacral masseuse who could get that calculator in his head to click off, and maybe if the linens were freshly laundered and the orange juice was freshly squeezed—maybe he would grin and bear it. But be sure not to overspend. That alone could ruin the whole trip!

Are you a night owl, dancing into the wee hours and drinking champagne from your slipper? *Get out of this relationship nowwwwwwwwww!!!!!!!!!* Mr. V's idea of a wild evening is a visit to the 7-Eleven to pick up some rust remover, so he can get a head start on the drain pipes in the morning. You'd enjoy picking the lint out of the dryer, wouldn't you? He thought so. Why not brew a cup of Ovaltine and spend a few challenging hours together hunting for every pesky speck of dust? *Wow!* After that you can both search for crumbs in the couch. He had no idea togetherness could be like this.

The Boy Scout of the zodiac, Mr. V's motto is "Be Prepared." Is he spending a romantic evening at your place? Check his briefcase. It will contain a travel alarm, razor, toothbrush, herbal dental floss, ginseng mouthwash, fresh underwear, plastic bag for dirty underwear, clean shirt, tie, socks, travel iron, wall plug for travel iron, condom, lubricant, ear plugs, digestive tablets, breath freshener, aspirin, Alka Seltzer, decongestant, and an herbal laxative, just in case. And you thought romance couldn't be planned in advance.

## ✴ How Virgo Likes His Women

Remember the three C's: cultivated, cultured, and civilized. Mr. V likes a beautifully mannered, poised woman who enjoys reading, thinking, and the art of good conversation. You take your time and do things right. You never blunder in the bedroom, the kitchen, or the office. You are thorough, reasonable, and wise. You have good taste. Your apartment could be photographed for a home magazine. You wear superb shoes at all times. Your stockings do not have runs. You understand a financial report, and your checkbook is a marvel of equilibrium. The IRS sends you thank-you notes at tax time.

## ✷ What Virgo Sees When He Looks At You

No matter if you sling hash at the Pit Stop Cafe; you are noble at heart. You have a quiet, refined, and classic air about you. Virgo likes a suggestion of breeding, a gracious woman who knows how to make others feel comfortable and at ease. Furthermore, you have soft, shiny hair that is beautifully cared for at all times; your nails are discreet perfection. You always smell of herbs and sunlight. You work out enough to maintain your figure, since he's into appearances—yours and his. He is always beautifully dressed and freshly scrubbed. You have a marvelous sensuality that is not sexual, not maternal, but comforting, earthy, and entirely your own. You are a woman a man could get lost in.

## ✷ What Turns Him On

Mr. V is attracted to a finely tuned wit. He likes mental stimulation first and foremost. Challenge him, let him make you laugh, and, above all, talk! Virgos are marvelous talkers. One Virgo/Aries couple we know ceased having sex (no chemistry), but stayed together for several years anyway for the sheer pleasure of the conversation.

## ✷ What Rules Virgo

A rage and passion for order. To feed this obsession, he will analyze and criticize and classify and categorize until he is satisfied, which is never. Your mission, should you wish to accept it, is to introduce him to the values of the human heart, the forgotten god in his pantheon.

## THE CHASE

### ✳ His Secret Paradox

The truth is, he's rather lonely. The problem is, no one knows this. Including him. He assumes that there is no one who could share his celestial inner sanctums, but he assumes wrong. Also, he imagines that his solitude is far preferable to the messy domestic situations he witnesses all around him. But he is wrong about this as well. Help him see that love can enrich his solitude, which you, the beloved, will cherish as much as he.

### ✳ How To Bewitch Virgo

This is tough. He can come across as positively seduction-proof to the unwary. So keep in mind the following points:

1. Challenge his keen, mentally agile intellect.
2. Virgos can dish with the best of them. Let yourself laugh at his devastatingly on-target appraisals.
3. Don't crowd him. You, possessive? You can't even spell the word.
4. Don't push the relationship too fast. Hint: of course, you believe that simple friendship between a man and a woman is possible.
5. Don't force monsieur to be a party animal. You, personally, prefer a good book to tiresome social affairs. In fact, you adore reading aloud to someone, but you can't find many people interested in such an old-fashioned pursuit.
6. Flaunt your other interests and pursuits, such as your job, your garden, and baking all your own

bread while listening to classical music.

7. Be comfortable around him—so comfortable, it's as if you've known him for years. Comfort is so essential, isn't it?

8. Do not be completely available. My God, he's fascinating to listen to. You wish you could stay longer, but work calls! Perhaps you could contact him next month for his opinion on the latest tax breaks?

## ✳ Don't . . .

Forget that his spice cabinet is alphabetized—do not place nutmeg next to basil. Squeeze his toothpaste tube in the middle. Bathe only twice a day. Leave a dish in the sink. Stop flossing. Leave newspapers on the floor. Use tap water in his iron. Run out of mouthwash. Be indecisive. Stop balancing your checkbook. Be two minutes late. Leave Marvel comics in the bathroom. Tell him you lied about your MBA. Make out with him at the checkout counter. Tell him that when you want his suggestions, you'll fax him. . . . (Feel perfectly free, however, to criticize!)

## ✳ Who He Likes To Bed

Witty, ambitious, attractive, fit, unpossessive women who like to flirt. Virgoman likes a good fling, and in his preoccupied life, there are many flings to be flung. If you're looking for good, clean fun—well, he's studiously good in bed, he's always clean, and he can be very funny—look no further. Just don't look to the future, because he may not be there.

### * Who He Likes To Wed

He does not. We're talking Bachelor Extraordinaire of the Zodiac here. Maybe if he's tired of all those flings. Maybe if there was a woman who wasted few words, who was quiet at just the right times. Maybe if she cooked blueberry pancakes to just the right consistency, and had a secret garden, and loved to listen. And had sufficient income. And knew where she was going. And loved to spend weekends reading Jane Austen. And always smelled like clouds in June. Maybe if he found a woman who knew that steaming vegetables instead of boiling them preserves their vitamin content. And who liked every room in the house to be delightfully comfortable. She who is the mate of his silent, secluded soul.

### * What He's Secretly Afraid Of

What if he got married and slowly died from the horror of having another person around, intruding on his sacred space, twenty-four hours a day, day in and day out? What if she left—shudder!— crumbs in the bed! Perfection is just a Platonic ideal. His Quicken program is beginning to look awfully romantic. Dirty sex is better. His breath mints aren't 100 percent effective. Neither is his deodorant.

### * When To Say Yes

Saying yes to a fling with Virgo is a snap. He's fun, he's witty, you're both adults, etc., etc. Marriagewise, if you get to yes with Mr. V you deserve the Ironman trophy. You will have been so exhaustively inspected, examined, investigated, probed and scrutinized, that only soul-searing love will carry you across that invisible threshold. On the other hand, if he proposes, you have every right to feel like the most distinctively unique woman in the world. You are.

## THE COUP DE GRACE

### ✷ His Sexual Secrets And Desires

Virgo is the original Frog Prince. Kiss him in the right way, at the right time, and he will blossom in ways you never dared dream. So be sure the wine is properly chilled and the bed is comfortably loaded with downy pillows and downier quilts. The room is the optimum temperature: not too cool, not too humid, not too dry, not too moist. There are flowers arranged simply, in an elegant vase. There is low, rhythmic music. You are wearing a beautiful silk robe that conceals your body, yet suggests—oh, how enchantingly—that you would be just as comfortable without it.

As you hand him a perfectly chilled glass of Chablis Grand Cru, stand behind his head and begin to gently knead the back of his neck. Use some eucalyptus balm and work your fingers deep into his shoulders. Now slowly move up his head, into his hair. Give him a slow scalp massage. When you are done, kiss him and tell him that you got massage oil all over his skin, and how would he like a bath? Tell him you've been dying to give him a bath, but you were too shy to bring it up. When he says yes (and with his passion for cleanliness, there will be no protest), gently take his wine, take him by the other hand, and lead him to the bathroom.

There, you have a pile of warmed bath sheets

waiting by the tub. The tub is half-filled with clean, green, scented bubbles. The lighting is soft, but not too dark. Put his wine down carefully, and ask him if you can undress him. Tell him you want to kiss him the entire time. Try to maintain mouth contact while you completely disrobe him. This will make him laugh and unbend yet further. When he is naked, ask him to step into the tub. Then gently begin to massage him with one of those huge sea sponges, with just a hint of honey-milled soap; don't overdo the soap. Lift his arms, wash his hands, his fingers, and then his chest. Go as slowly as possible.

Now stop. Tell him there's something you've forgotten. Stand up and let your robe fall to the floor. Climb into the tub, and sit gently on his chest. Taking a washcloth, wet his hair all over. Now, with lingering, prolonged fingerstrokes, give him a slow, sensual shampoo. Kiss him in time to your strokes. Tell him you're getting turned on. Ask him if he can help you. Without stopping your fingers, lift yourself onto his erect penis and continue your massage. Let your fingers and your vagina massage him in the same slow, sensuous rhythms. Don't stop. When you feel yourself about to come, tell him. Ask him to kiss you. Lean down and kiss his mouth as you let yourself explode, riding him in the rhythms of the warm, green water. He should not be coherent for quite a while.

## ✳ Shhh!

Definitely seduce him in a public place sometime. A garage, the subway, an airplane ... introduce him to the ecstasies of surrender to the moment, something he has never heard of. But since he hates public displays of affection, make sure no one's looking. The tension will make him explode, and he will be starry-eyed.

## AFTERGLOW: WHAT YOU NEED TO KNOW

### ✱ What Virgo Likes Better Than Sex

Analyzing. Diagnosing. Evaluating. He calls it stimulating. You may call it tedious.

### ✱ Will He Marry His Best Lover Or Best Friend?

This man will definitely marry a friend, an equal, and a partner. However, she is a friend who has magnificently seduced him and opened his eyes to the possibilities of (shhh!) lust. In fact, he never knew he had a body until he met her.

### ✱ What He Wants From You

Mental challenges and stimulation. To the French, conversation is as important as sexual skill. Maybe more so. (The sun sign of Paris is Virgo.) So bear this in mind. Virgo adores the exhilaration of clever dialogue and sparkling repartee. Also, it is second nature to Virgo to worry about what people will say. Thus, he wants you to reflect his worth in the eyes of the world. And finally, Mr. V wants and needs your restful, sensual presence to help him climb down from his personal Tower of Babylon at the end of the day. Become his relaxation response, and he will stay by your side til the end of your days.

### ✳ What He Needs From You

To feel safe. In order for Virgo to open up and share his life, he needs to feel that his privacy is sacred to you, and that you will guard it always with your love. Also, since he suffers more from his critical faculties than anyone else (yes, he does), he has a hard time feeling truly worthy. What he needs from you is to be needed. Not taken advantage of, but needed. Show him that you need him, precisely because you, too, are a very private person, and you will continue to need him for the rest of your remarkable life together.

### ✳ What He Won't Give Up For You

One-third of his privacy. If he is setting up house with you, you have been admitted to the holy of holies—His Daily Routine. For this you deserve a life achievement award. Feel deeply honored, because he won't give up anything else. (As a toddler, your Virgin got stuck in the anal phase of development, thus causing him lifelong problems with release.)

### ✳ What He Will Give Up For You

Give UP? He—gasp! he might be having an asthma attack here; hold on—he needs to *give up something??* He will *rearrange* his daily routines, he will divide the space in his vitamin closet, and he will get you your own mouthwash, soap, toothpaste, and pillow. And towels. And washcloth. And shampoo. And conditioner. Possibly, there could be two toilet-paper dispensers so you wouldn't have to share. He unrolls his a special way, you see.

There's a reason why Virgos have a hard time getting—and sometimes staying—married.

## ✳ How To Make Him Fall In Love With You, Really

Mr. V considers the intellect by far his most significant asset. It is your job to introduce him to that seismograph in his chest. Teach him that he has a heart, and that when the heart comes first, all his careful routines will fall into beautiful order. Show him that there is a higher law than logical reasoning, and that humans who discover this higher law lead much more fulfilling lives. And last, show him in deeply private, personal language that the heart has eyes, is not blind, and knows what it wants. By this time, what his heart will want is you.

## ✳ Make It Forever

Never lie about yourself, since Virgo sees through all artifice quicker than anyone alive. And learn to love him because of, not in spite of, his rabbit warren of routines, programs, systems, and methods. He is a kind, loving, thoughtful man who badly needs to be understood and admired for his shining qualities, and not everyone can do this. His love goes deeper and lasts longer than many more passionate, hotter males. And for the right woman, Virgo is the truly perfect mate.

Finally, your Virgo is in grave danger of missing the forest for the trees. How can he raise his eyes to heaven when there are all those weeds to be pulled? Gently suggest that if you examine Monet's *Waterlilies* up close—too close—it's just tiny, messy blobs of paint. Only perspective can give him the beauty and the glory of art. And life. And you.

# CRUCIAL MINUTIAE

## * What To Feed Virgo

Digestive biscuits. Seriously soothing food. Virgo can develop major stomach problems from nerves and worry. All types of soups, from squash to homemade chicken, will pacify his hypersensitive metabolism. Herbal teas, especially those with medicinal qualities, will do nicely, particularly if they're served in big, sparkling white mugs with a pressed napkin and a plate for the tea bag. Make sure he gets lots of crisp, carefully washed salads dressed with balsamic or poppy-seed vinaigrette. And don't forget the bran—homemade, sugarless oat-bran muffins, breads, and cookies will all please his fussy palate. Virgo needs help occasionally in letting go of life's more intractable problems.

## * How To Take Care Of Your Virgo

Peace. Think peace and quiet, two pillars of Virgoan desire. Kidnap him to a safe, serene spot (it could be your apartment) and have a plump teapot ready, full of fresh mint (for his stomach) and chamomile (for his nerves). Listen to him until he talks himself down and out of his frenetic, agitated state. Take a course in reflexology, and massage the pressure points on his feet, thus releasing toxins and relaxing him at the same time—a perfect Virgo experience.

Tai Chi is ideal for Virgo, inducing tranquility, balance, and long life with its ancient Chinese wisdom. Don't forget to take him for long walks in the park or the country. And lastly, learn the art of being there, just being there for him. It will teach him and amaze him more than anything else you will ever do.

## ✳ For His Birthday

Consider one of those pocket computers that will hold 5,000 names and addresses, calculate physics problems, tell the time in six zones, hook up to a printer, and fax for him without dialing. Of course, he wants the model with the long-term alarm clock that can be set five months ahead to remind him of special events. Virgo would also appreciate a white-noise machine, which masks sounds, for a good night's sleep.

Out of ideas? Try a great lecture series on art or religion, taped so that he can listen to it in his car, thus learning as he drives. Books are always welcome to the Virgin, as are tickets to lectures or a concert. How about a personal sterilizer to render his private utensils germfree? Or a box of worry dolls? Made in Mexico, these are five or six tiny dolls that you place under your pillow, where they supposedly do all your worrying for you while you sleep. Better get him a case.

○ ◖●◗ ) ☽

*Frederick 10-14-63*
*Jim Kelly 10-15-46*

# libra

## SEPTEMBER 24 · OCTOBER 23

### BEST LOVE MATCHES

Libra & Gemini
Libra & Leo
Libra & Aquarius

He's witty, he's graceful, and his charm could cause a nuclear meltdown. He's amusing a crowd of beautiful people, and his smile could steal your heart. He's Libra, the Scales.

## FAMOUS LIBRANS

Jeremy Irons, Armand Assante, Luke Perry, John Lennon, Michael Crichton, Bruce Springsteen, Ralph Lauren, Christopher Reeve, Luciano Pavarotti, Sting

## I AM

Having an utterly marvelous time. I adore parties. What more perfect arena to indulge my twin cravings for sparkling debate and beautiful women?

I've been told I spend my life in pursuit of Truth
and Beauty; that sounds much too energetic. I
wouldn't say I pursue Beauty—but with you sitting
before me it's getting harder and harder to think. I
cannot abide ugliness. Even if I had to live in a
garage, it would have to be a quaint, landmark garage made of fieldstone and oak. Beauty is harmony, and harmony keeps my raging passions in
balance. You don't think I have raging passions?
You think this lazy smile and this languid pose are
as frisky as I get? My dear, where are your eyes?
You disappoint me!

And do I seek Truth? I seek decisions; but no
decision is final until I have looked at it from at
least nineteen sides. Thus my decisions take time.
Lots of time. Perhaps I do seek Truth, just to verify
my reality. Would you say reality is verifiable? But
there I go again! I live for discussions like this!

Unpleasant people would say I live to argue, but
how unfair that is. Argument involves aggression,
and I am never aggressive. What I am after is the
exhilaration of debate, the stimulus of the moment.
If I seem to be winning too easily, sometimes I
switch sides, just for the sheer thrill of arguing
against myself. I do need to win, at all costs. But I
need win fairly, at all costs. You see the dilemma.
I always do, and therefore I keep on talking until
fairness, and harmony, and my point of view pre-
vail.

I have an intense need to share my life—not
dominate, not submit, not control, not obey, but
share. Just watching you like this is putting a spell
on me. I'm already half in love. I can't help it! And
we haven't even been introduced.

I'm very interested in you. But should I wait? Is

the moment right? It is! No. Perhaps I should linger; perhaps I should watch you interact with other men. But that's crazy! You're enchanting me! Should I move? Should I stay?

The world thinks I live in the clouds—the world is wrong. Dreams are real, and the secret to making them real is to never stop dreaming. Come and look at the moon with me and I'll explain how it works. But you have stolen my heart, and I don't even know your name! Will you come? Will you give me that heart-stopping smile and come?

## YOU ARE

A gloriously feminine woman with a first-class brain. And in you, beauty and brains are a perfect pair. And yes, you are beautiful. I can't help it! I adore beautiful women! Yet even though you may have unconventional beauty, you appreciate your uniqueness and emphasize it at all times. Your hair is a radiant waterfall; your skin is like a Vermeer. Your posture reminds me of Grace Kelly in *The Philadelphia Story*; God knows how you learned to move like that, but don't ever stop.

You are secure enough to relish the entire range of feminine expression. I love perfume, furs, elegant heels, bustiers, diamonds, the occasional baby-doll dress, lipstick, bikinis—I love women who enjoy being women. And you obviously do.

You project the profound calm of an afternoon sea; emotional dramas amuse you—in others. You have a clearheaded, stable approach to the world, with a lovely, rational optimism that I rely on more than you know. Your home reflects this inner harmony. You have the gift of creating tranquility around you, and your taste is second to none. With your choice of flowers, color, and music, you weave a web of peace and symmetry that mesmerizes me; your home gives me that feeling of serenity that I don't seem to be able to give to myself.

The greatest talent you possess, however, is your ability to be there, always, in the center of my soul, while I roam my private mental range. I need freedom—mental and sometimes emotional—and you understand that with a depth that needs no words. In return, I bring you all the gifts of my mind and heart, and lay them at your feet.

## HOW TO DRIVE ME WILD

Make it subtle. I'll pick up every cue you send me. Know that rules are for breaking, and that limits don't interest me.

I adore that perfume. It's so light I barely know it's there. And pearls—nice. Women in pearls demand the best service. And those stockings! Where did you get seamed stockings? I like the way you're keeping things open—your mouth, your legs, your . . . was that a hint of white silk garter? Pretend you don't know I'm watching. Pretend you're not turning me on to the point where I barely know what I'm saying.

Now take off your blouse. Slowly. Strip for me. Leave the G-string. Look at me while you do it. I want you to use your mouth on my body. Softly. Use your lips on my face. I want your tongue all over my body. All over, do you understand? But take your time. Suck on my nipples; that's good. Let your tongue graze my navel. No, don't touch my balls yet. Don't hurry me. I don't like that.

Stop. Look at me. Tell me exactly what you want me to do to you. You know I like to please. Pleasing

you makes me hot. Do you want me to take your
nipples in my mouth? Do you want me to suck on
them? Do you like it soft or hard? Do you want me
to kiss you thighs—and all the other delicious parts
of you? How? Long, slow strokes? Use my whole
tongue? I won't let up until you tell me every single
thing you want. I want to see you blush. I want to
see you get embarrassed and ask for it anyway. Do
you want me inside you? How? Fast and hard?
Slow and easy?

That's good. That's very good. Now use your
tongue on my balls. Gently. Show me how much
you want me. Tell me you want me. Now let me
feel your tongue on my penis. Softly! Little licks,
gentle licks. Barely there. Let me feel them. Tell me
what you want me to do to you. I didn't hear that.
Tell me exactly what you want. Now take me in
your mouth. Don't stop those gentle, tiny licks.
Don't stop teasing me. Yes, like that. Don't stop.
Don't. Stop.

## CONFIDENTIALLY YOURS

### ✳ What He Won't Tell You

To be or not to be? That is the question. Well, that
is one of the questions he'll keep asking until an
answer finally appears and puts him out of his misery. Bet you didn't know Hamlet was a Libra. The
guy was witty, literate, erudite, and polished. Also
indecisive, ambivalent, romantically shallow, and a
world-class procrastinator. Also in love with
words, in love with himself—and charming as hell.
If that isn't a flawless portrait of Mr. Scales, we'll
eat our Shakespeare.

Libra is the original Iron Fist in the Velvet Glove.

His determination to get what he wants would bore holes through solid granite. Behind all that French Vanilla charm, there's a cold, logical scientist rearranging the pieces on the chessboard. So don't be fooled by the dreamy romanticism, the gentle promise to be fair. He's excruciatingly fair—to himself. If there's any fairness left over, why, be his guest.

You should note, however, that he's never aggressive. Libra is horrified at aggressive behavior—his own and everyone else's. He likes to believe he's enchanting. He will enchant you to his will and pleasure, and you will be so mesmerized you'll give in and apologize for taking so long.

Furthermore, he takes three years to make up his mind. Don't take him to a restaurant with long menus; you'll starve to death before the order is taken. Never take him into the video store to choose the movie; make him wait in the car. And have the phrase, "On the other hand" tatooed on your fanny. This way he will feel right at home during lovemaking.

Psst! It's not that Libra cannot resist an argument; it's that he cannot resist *taking the other side*. Life can be a bowl of cherries once you grasp this tiny fact. Whenever he's mad at you, tell him what a dreadfully naughty, thoughtless, lowly worm you have been. He'll burst a blood vessel proving how adorable, perfect, and angelic you really are, and how thrilled he is just to be near you. Mr. Impartial Objectivity has to win, you see. So make sure he wins in your favor. And don't forget to tell him how persuasive he is.

Does he care what the neighbors think? *Mais oui!* And the neighbor's dog, and the local librarian, and the guy who polishes his shoes, and the astronauts up in space and all those beings he assumes live on Mars and stare down at him, nightly, grading his performance.

This is part of the reason that Libra tends to be a little, shall we say, self-absorbed. And Libra does not have the self-absorption of an ordinary mortal. He has the self-absorption of the artist, which he considers not self-absorption, but Art. As Merlin was imprisoned in an enchanted cave, so Libra is imprisoned in an enraptured world of Beauty, Love, Poetry, and Centerfolds.

That's why if you are a living, breathing woman with real emotional needs, you may be another thing entirely to Mr. Scales: in the way. He's deeply engrossed in the most marvelous daydream—and you're breathing all over it. Could you breathe over there, please? Many thanks.

## ✱ The Bad Stuff

I justify, therefore I am.

Can charm be a registered weapon? No, but in his case, they're making an exception. And is it love or a figment of his imagination? He doesn't know. Does it matter? Yes. He'd prefer the figment, since figments don't have hysterics or bad-hair days, or spill nail polish all over his pillow.

He's deeply touched by Beauty, and deeply repelled by Ugliness, which causes him to feel existential nausea. When young and immature, Libra often confuses the skin-deep for the soul-deep. To maintain ideal conditions, all you have to do is look stunningly beautiful at 5:00 A.M., when the cat has thrown up all over the bed, and again at 7:15 A.M., when the alarm clock has failed to go off. Battle enlarged pores. Drink parsley juice to prevent water weight. Brush those perfect little pearl-like teeth. And spare two hours a day for the gym—you wouldn't want to put him off his feed, now would you?

Want to play house? OK. You empty the cat litter and scrub the toilet, and he'll arrange the flowers on the mantelpiece. What! You object? But his aesthetic sensibilities cannot be confronted with anything so unkind as cat litter! Surely you jest!

Mr. Scales is happiest with a partner who has a trace of Brunhilda in her—she who will scrub the tub, tell the guests to go home already, and get him out of having dinner with his brother-in-law. His job is to soak long and hard in the bath, charm the pants off the guests, and smile lovingly at his brother-in-law. From afar.

When it's time for sex, be prepared for a barrage of questions. Did the earth move for you, too? Really? Was it as good as last time? What else would you like? More oral sex? Another orgasm? What else could he do to make you happy? The good news is that, with his need to please, Libra will fret over your pleasure. But with his equally pressing need to push all inquiries over the edge, you frequently wish he'd shaddup already and leave you to it. Some things do not need to be excessively catalogued.

One reason for the fact that Libra often marries late is the well-hidden set of apron strings tied around his middle. Unlike Cancer, who talks to Mom in his sleep, Libra will never breathe a word about her. Yet this dazzlingly desirable guy is often a momma's boy in disguise. So his ideal partner had better be stable, assertive, and in control of her life. And nurturing, peaceful, and totally understanding. And take care of his dirty socks, leaky faucet, and all those distasteful dishes in the sink. Furthermore, she should let him wander at will, but she should be there, waiting for him, when he chooses to come home. WHO DOES THIS SOUND LIKE? Ask him about his mother sometime. He'll either adore her or hate her. (It's the same thing.) But he won't be neutral.

Ah, temper. He was hoping you wouldn't inquire about that nasty little word. Do not stir the dark waters of Charm Boy's wrath. It is a black, nasty, and possibly violent experience. When Libra gets mad, the best policy is to run, so that you may return again to play another day.

## ✳ How Libra Likes His Women

You are a strong, assertive, magnetic woman who stimulates his intellect night and day. You have a marvelous sense of humor. You get what you want, yet you are so appealing that you disarm your opponents with wit and charm. You never argue to dominate; you argue for the sheer joy of stretching your mind.

Although you are sophisticated, you have a pleasing simplicity that enthralls him. Are you a physicist or a color consultant? You could be either, since you're intelligent enough for ten men and seductive enough for twenty. You could be both, since conventional roles bore you to death. You have a deep understanding of the word "partner." You may be his true love, but you are also his equal, his peer, and his match. Furthermore, you have your own need for mental and emotional space, and so you grant him the space he so desperately needs in equal measure. Why not? It's only fair.

## ✳ What Libra Sees When He Looks At You

You have marvelous taste in clothes, which kindles his imagination. You always manage to look as if you've just come back from safari, or apple-picking, or a country dance. You have splendid, carefully brushed hair, which you wear in romantically simple styles. You have a forceful personality, yet you look terrific in a gauze skirt. With bare feet. And a little-nothing top. You have that indescribable air—perhaps a forgotten corner of your soul is always somewhere else. He's not sure, but he is enraptured as he seeks to penetrate your mystery.

Furthermore, you are serenity itself. There is peace and stillness in your smile, in your eyes, and in the way you look at him across a room. When deeply moved, you do not scream, faint, or throw things. And, last but never least, you have a marvelous sexuality that is utterly available to him—and no one else!

## ✳ What Turns Him On

Intellectual challenge. If you don't feel up to it, read the newspaper and ask him a leading question. Or, if you're feeling daring, take a really forceful stand on something: are women stronger than men? should people marry before 30? The stronger the stand, the better. He will spring to the challenge—verbal contests are his favorite drug. Show off your independent, reflective, strong-minded brain. But show it off in the most alluring way. These are not life-and-death issues; you're just having fun sparring with an intellectual equal. Laughing, you bend over to pick up your napkin. You're not wearing a bra.

## * What Rules Libra

Dialogue—it's his middle name. Libra defines who
he is by his neverending argument with the world.
Never forget that monsieur needs to express himself *constantly*. Remember Roger Rabbit, who would
rather face death than miss a chance to vocalize?
Roger Rabbit was a Libra.

# THE CHASE

## * His Secret Paradox

Libra's whole personality is based on paradox. He
seeks fairness, but has to win. He champions truth,
but beauty can upset his applecart quicker than a
jump in the hay. He needs close partnership, but
lots of space. He craves true harmony and the ultimate high. His ultimate paradox? He wants to be
balanced, yet he wants you to do it for him. But
not until he does it himself will he achieve the
peace he's looking for.

## * How To Bewitch Libra

Unlike Virgo, it's not too difficult. Bewitched, be-
mused and bedazzled is his preferred emotional
mode. Praise him as he praises others. Libra loves
to have his skills and achievements noticed, even
the small ones. Especially the small ones, because
he's not sure they're important.

Engage him in discussion, and, while talking,
look at him and mentally picture just exactly what
you'd like to do to him. In great detail. Keep conversing. Keep imaging. Keep conversing. Keep imaging. See if you can get him to get an erection by
your mental stimulation alone. Give no hint that

this is what you are doing. At the perfect moment, break off the argument, er, conversation, and leave. Say goodbye and walk out the door. Walk very slowly—and don't look back.

## ✳ Don't . . .

Play heavy metal during dinner. Forget to shower. Forget to wear makeup. Paint the bedroom bright red. Paint anything bright red. Tell him you have an unlimited checking account. Tell him you have unlimited anything relating to money. Tell him little orgasms are just fine, thanks. Ask him to take care of the details. Flirt. Ask how much dinner cost. Tell him to hurry up already with his orgasm; you have a breakfast meeting.

## ✳ Who He Likes To Bed

You are his aphrodisiac. You are a passionate woman who likes philosophizing, especially when naked. You love the arts—especially the erotic ones. You like to follow pleasure down whatever dark and mysterious path it may lead you—and "enough" is not a word in your vocabulary. You believe too much of a good thing is absolutely wonderful, whether it's one more Bellini or one more orgasm before dawn. You wear the unmistakable look of a woman who adores the boudoir, and every secret thing that transpires within.

## ✳ Who He Likes To Wed

Romance and love are two different animals. The first one eats you alive; the second can feed you forever. Libra needs to learn the ins and outs of the second kind of love—real love—that gets up in the morning and takes out the garbage and butters the toast and finds joy in the little daily things of life.

Luckily for you, he doesn't really want Mom—he just wants all her good qualities grafted onto the wittiest, most seductive girl in the world. Libra is drawn to strong women who project emotional stability (we didn't say they had it; we said they project it)—who are also funny, idiosyncratic, and have learned the impossible trick of living daily life in the most stimulating, romantic way.

## ✶ What He's Secretly Afraid Of

Possibly he has failed to please you. Possibly he has failed to please the local dry cleaner. All that whispering is about his numerous social failures. Charm is skin-deep. Women prefer the strong, silent type (especially silent). It's laziness, not creative daydreaming. To find your soulmate, you have to have a soul. Grown-ups actually enjoy delayed gratification.

## ✶ When To Say Yes

Unfortunately, you may have said yes before you said hello. (Remember that deadly smile.) Libra will court and charm you to a dazzling build-up. Then he will gaze into the middle distance as he makes up his mind: Is this it? Is it time? Now? Are you the one? Or not?

Do *not* hit him over the head with the champagne bottle. Forcing him into a commitment (or even a date) will only get you a hairy eyeball and breath of steel. Best to make a decision of your own, as you glance at your watch and find, to your shock, that it's way past your bedtime! It's been dazzling, but you really must be home by midnight! Off you

trot, home to Fido and a good mystery novel! Now
count how many nanoseconds it takes him to make
up his mind about whether he wants you or not.

## THE COUP DE GRACE

### ✴ His Sexual Secrets And Desires

He wants to explode with pleasure. He wants to
flash into hyperspace with desire. Is there a sensation he hasn't experienced? Is there an erotic vari-
ation he has yet to encounter? Give it to him and
you'll hold his interest—and more.

Libra adores the aesthetic, sensual possibilities of
bathing. Let the lights be low; let there be candlelight flickering in all the rooms. Music is important:
a slow, rhythmic tempo that captures the mood.
Open a bottle of Roderer Cristalle and pour it into
two Baccarat flutes. Hand him one as you offer him
a plate of taste sensations: small black olives, imported cheese, focaccia dipped in aioli. Have a plate
of chocolate truffles nearby. Wear a silk robe that
is just a little see-through.

As you progress into the picnic, let your robe fall
partly open as you pick up a chocolate truffle,
which you delicately wet and smear on your nipples, going in slow, deliberate circles. When you
finish one nipple, do the other. Ask him to taste it.
When he leans in, run your finger down his chest,
leaving a smear of chocolate. When he licks you
clean, do the same for him.

Tell him you'd like to get really clean. Drop your
robe, disappear into the bathroom, and tell him to
bring the champagne. When he enters, there are
gorgeous deep-pile towels, a scented bath, and
hand-milled soap. Invite him into the tub. Slowly

massage his nipples with massage oil. Descending down his body, stroke his penis slowly with oil.

Tell him you love nudity. You've always wanted to be completely nude. It's so much more visually aesthetic. You'd love to feel yourself completely naked against his skin, his groin, his mouth. Would he, could he, shave you? Hand him a razor. You've always wanted a man to do this. Hand him some wonderfully scented shaving cream, and towels. When he begins to slide the razor over you, tell him it feels like he's caressing you. Tell him he's making you go hot by his strokes. Hold a hand mirror so you can watch his every move. Tell him it's like he's making love to you. You can't wait to feel his mouth on your lips.

When he's done, ask him to carry you to the bedroom, where there are at least six mirrors facing the bed. Shove him gently onto his back and ask him if you can sit on his face. Don't sit there immediately. Slide yourself slowly up his body, lingering on his penis and his chest. When you finally reach his face, hold yourself over his mouth while you ask him if he likes you like this. Ask him again. Ask him if he'd like to kiss you. Slowly, slowly lower yourself onto his mouth.

Begin to move very, very slowly. Let yourself explode in his mouth. Now slide back down, very slowly, onto his waiting penis. Tell him his balls feel amazing against your new nakedness. Slowly move in a rocking motion. Ask him to look at the two of you in the mirror. Ask him to please make you come so hard you'll pass out. Now. You want it now. Right now....

## * Shhh . . .

Have photographs of yourself taken in nothing but heels and pearls. Send them to his office by Federal Express, marked STRICTLY CONFIDENTIAL.

# AFTERGLOW: WHAT YOU NEED TO KNOW

## * What Libra Likes Better Than Sex

Not much. But debating wins by a nose. Self-expressing is deep in this man's DNA. Winning at self-expressing is even deeper in his DNA. Therefore, all your intellectual victories over Libra will be hollow at best. Remember this the next time you feel like beating him in an argument.

## * Will He Marry His Best Lover Or Best Friend?

His best lover, who is also his true, one and only partner, mate, peer, and friend. She also happens to be his romantic ideal of womanhood, compared with which Guinevere, Helen of Troy and Juliette are mere shadows.

## * What He Wants From You

You give great face. You also give great legs, breasts, and thighs. Not to mention superb mental stimulation. Exhilarating dialogue. Bosom thrills. Erotic adventures, in which you often lead. He also wants you very there when he needs you, very not there when he doesn't. This is peachy with you, since you're the same way.

## * What He Needs from You

An even keel. Harmony. Strength. Also great amounts of affection and joy in your companionship. He's, um, kind of dependent, actually. He often suffers a strange fear of abandonment, but if he learns day by day of your steadfastness and love, he may become secure enough to let go of the old, dark patterns. Then your love can grow into something truly wonderful and rare.

### ✳ What He Won't Give up For You

Charming every human being within shouting distance. Rising to the challenge—of debate, that is. Defending the underdog, defending the unwashed, defending any stray cause that no one has noticed recently. Asking for approval from all beings that breathe. Trying to satisfy the needs of people he hasn't met yet. Trying to make everyone get along. Burning the candle at three ends. *Taking ten years to make up his mind.*

### ✳ What He Will Give up For You

His fantasy of Eternal Womanhood, with whom he has been in love since birth. And if you are indeed she who provides him with a warm and loving, harmonious home, then he will relinquish the need to test-drive his seductive skills on half the human race. Libraman is very accommodating and not prone to tantrums over territory and identity, like some we could mention. He makes a marvelous feminist without losing an iota of his masculine appeal.

### ✳ How to Make Him Fall in Love With You, Really

1. Get him to defend you to yourself. This is easily accomplished by making righteous, self-

deprecating statements with just a hint of a challenge in there somewhere.

2. Libra's a pleaser, and he needs feedback. Congratulate him at least once a day on something he's done that no one has noticed.

3. Need him. He needs you to need him. So find yourself leaning toward him emotionally in a delightfully scary way.

4. Show him that there will be spaces in your togetherness, in the most comfortable way imaginable. You adore him; yet you are definitely not joined at the hip.

5. Surrender to his charm! It's lethal! It's terminal! It's paradise!

## ✷ Make It Forever

Libras are gentle and understanding, and make marvelous husbands, when well-mated. Make sure he knows that you love him not only for his dazzling performances in front of friends and peers, but that you love him all alone in a darkened room on a rainy day, when he is being particularly impossible. You may disagree with him; in fact, he's counting on you to disagree—where else would he get fuel for discussion? But you love him, completely, and that will never change.

For all his expressiveness, Libra tends to stutter when speaking the simple, illogical language of the heart. Feelings are the one thing he can't argue into the ground. So kiss him long and softly, and give him a framed engraving that reads "The heart has its reasons, which reason doesn't understand." Hang it somewhere in the bedroom. Repeat it softly every so often, especially when he gets that lost look, which means his feelings are out of control.

Love is not control. Love is what you feel. Make it safe for him to know this.

## CRUCIAL MINUTIAE

### ✳ What To Feed Libra

Beautifully prepared, elegantly served, exquisitely proportioned food. Exquisite proportion is important, since (1) aesthetics is all to this man and (2) you want to help him watch his tendency to overindulge. Don't just hand him an orange. Peel it for him, and arrange the slices in a star pattern on a blue Delft plate, with a linen napkin and a glass of Perrier. Feed all his five senses at once—that's the secret Libran formula for pleasure. Breakfast in bed? He'll swoon. But make it fresh strawberries with Devonshire cream, and homemade brioche with clover honey, served on antique Majolica. Hand him a sterling silver spoon to stir his espresso. Libra would turn life into art on a daily basis, if he could. Indulge this tendency when nurturing him, and he will come back forever more.

### ✳ How to Take Care Of Your Libra

Naps! Catnaps! Siestas! Sneak-a-Snooze! Bedtime stories! He's a workaholic who parties hearty, so Libraman needs R & R more than any other guy in the zodiac. Make sure he gets lots of it. His mind is a nuclear seesaw, and it never stops. Introduce him to the tranquility of meditation; have a space in your apartment just for sitting. Have music that is just for relaxing, and play it often—especially when he's in danger of burnout. Massage is a must:

slow Swedish strokes all over his tensed-up torso
will have him disencumbering in no time.

## ✳ For His Birthday

It's the thought that counts with this man. But if
the gift happens to be something elegant and one-
of-a-kind, he's in heaven. Give him a hammock,
complete with stand, blanket, and wonderful old
novel. No place for a hammock? Try a Sky Chair
(a canvas seat that hangs from the ceiling and
makes you feel as if you are floating on air)—perfect for the charismatic daydreamer who's thinking
up his next novel. Tickets to a play, movie, or museum exhibit will always please; Libra is artistically
inclined. In fact, give him art—an original painting,
sculpture, or pen-and-ink wash that spoke to you.
He will be seriously thrilled, and his opinion of
your taste will rise exponentially.

# scorpio

## OCTOBER 24 - NOVEMBER 22

### BEST LOVE MATCHES

Scorpio & Cancer
Scorpio & Capricorn
Scorpio & Pisces

He's up on the balcony, away from the crowd. He prefers life and love one-on-one. His eyes could burn right through you. He's intense. He's legendary. He's Scorpio, the Scorpion.

## FAMOUS SCORPIOS

Pablo Picasso, Dostoyevsky, David Schwimmer, Bill Gates, Calvin Klein, Ted Turner, Prince Charles, Adam Horovitz, Jason Alexander, Jeff Goldblum, Sinbad

## I AM

Watching. . . . I prefer being up here, out of sight, where I can monitor the human comedy below. I have few close friends, to whom I am intensely devoted. Our host at this party is a close friend of mine—therefore, I am here.

But I find social gatherings shallow; I have no desire to penetrate the mind of anyone who can stand around and waste time yakking to perfect strangers. Penetrating the mind is what I live for. You're probably wondering at such words coming from a quiet, unassuming man. Excuse my dark glasses; I use them to keep the inquisitive away. But back to the mind—the supreme source of power. Information is power, and the information I prize most highly lies buried deep in the minds of other people.

Have you concluded that I was born without a sense of humor? You conclude wrong. I admire wit, cleverness, repartee. But life is profoundly serious to me, and I loathe wasted time. I will be controlling the company I work for in a very short time; not everyone may know who's running the shop, however. I see no need to advertise my power. It is enough that I have it.

I'd prefer to be home, alone, with a good book, but now that I'm here I want to know who you are. You seem to put a spell on everyone you meet. You do it perfectly—the exquisite politeness, the ever-so-slight boredom, the genuinely friendly, genuinely unromantic pose . . . it's good. It's very good. Forgive me for seeing right through you, but I see right through everyone. You have tremendous personal power; so do I. I think it's time we met.

You'd probably like me to explain myself. Forget

about it. I have a bulletproof psyche, and no one gets through without my permission. I give nothing away. Absolutely nothing. One of my secret pleasures is to infiltrate the mind and soul of another, while remaining invisible to them. In fact, I'd love to be invisible at will.

I am into spiritual truth—my own and everyone else's. I expect you to live up to your word, your divine purpose, and to the spirit, if not the letter, of the law. If you fail—well, you are human, but it's far better to personally experience your mistakes. That way you never forget the lesson. And I just happen to be an expert at helping people experience their mistakes. I am not into revenge, as some have snidely suggested. Who would call what I do revenge? It is metaphysical balancing, in its purest form. And it is one of my purposes on Earth.

If I want you, no barrier will exist to me. I have unlimited stamina; I have an unbreakable will. I have never failed to get what I truly desire. Do not resist me; there is literally nowhere you can hide.

But don't be frightened. So many foolish people are frightened of me. I need someone who can accept the full depth of my love, to whom I can devote myself with all the intensity of my soul. I am looking for the woman who is worthy of my fidelity, since once I have found her, I will never look at another.

Although I would never admit this to a living soul, I have enormous emotional needs, and I seek the company of someone with whom I can at last be myself. I have a heart that is as vast as the midnight sky, and a need to devote myself to a great love. Are you the one? Can you withstand my emotional power? Have you, perhaps, been looking for me too ?

I think it's time we met.

# YOU ARE

She who sees through me. I am a born schemer; my social machinations would put the Borgias to shame. But I never scheme around you; I wouldn't dare. You're too smart and too wise to put up with it, and, unlike me, you have a wonderful absence of emotional cunning. One of the many things I cherish about you is the steadfast loyalty of your heart.

You are one seriously sexy woman. I am a dominant, strong-willed man, and I need a woman who understands the spiritual and sensual joy of submission. While we have an equal partnership, there are still ancient mysteries between a man and a woman that need to be honored in private, and I don't need to explain that any further.

And finally, home is where your heart is. Mine, too. I love few things better than to watch you curled up by a cozy fire in your immaculate living room, sipping a glass of mulled wine and listening to music. You value the privacy of our love; you are not a social butterfly, thank God, but an exquisitely sensitive woman who reveals herself only to a well-chosen few. You are the only woman in the world to whom I can devote myself completely, without reservation, and I will move heaven and earth—and hell, if necessary—to make you mine.

# HOW TO DRIVE ME WILD

Make out with me with your eyes. Do you want me? Let it show. I like that bodysuit you're wearing. You're not afraid to show off. Good. Keep looking at me. I have a need to completely dominate you—you know that, don't you? That's what you're here for. In my secret heart I long for some-

one to possess me, body and soul, but I'm afraid
no one ever will, and I don't know that I'd let her.

You convey that you know . . . things. That
drives me crazy. You give good eye. What else do
you give? Take off your clothes. Let me watch.
Don't be modest, there is no room between us for
modesty. Walk around the room. Slowly. Bend
over and pick up that glass of wine. Good. Now
come undress me. Kiss me while you're undressing
me. I want you to use me to turn yourself on. Lie
on top of me and slide your body up and down.
That's it. Dance on top of me. Use the music. Touch
me with your vagina. See if you can kiss me like
that, just with your lips. That's right. Kiss the tip
of my penis with your vagina.

Tell me what you feel. Dance on the top of me.
Now I'm going to finger you while you do that,
and you're going to let me. You're going to let me
finger you and squeeze your nipples, just like this,
just enough so you feel it. A hint of pain makes the
pleasure more intense. Do you like what I'm doing
to you? Later I want you to wear these nipple rings
for me. I want you to wear the mark of my slave.
Just for tonight. Do you want that? Let me hear
you. Show me. Slide over me. That's it. Swallow
me up. Yes. Feel my fur against your belly. Let it
go. Let it all go. I'm fingering you, and I want you
aroused, very aroused. Give yourself to me. I want
you to come now. Now. Give it all to me. That's
right. Don't it hold back. Let me hear you. Louder.
Scream. Louder. *Louder. Now!*

# CONFIDENTIALLY YOURS

### ✳ What He Won't Tell You

His friends call him Silent-But-Deadly behind his back. Both of them.

He's dark, he's deep, he broods, he sighs, he wrestles with God in his spare time. Enough already. For sheer, seething morbidity, Scorpster gets the Edgar Allan Poe award. Prepare yourself for extended periods when Old Cyberface communes with himself and his Maker. That grinding noise is his soul, writhing in existential torment. Call him "Edgar" once in a while. When the brooding gets obsessive, buy him a raven.

Scorpio assumes he gives nothing away. It's true that you have to chisel a smile out of his granite facade, but the Scorpion is easier to read than you think. He may think he's stone-faced, but he seethes with passion. He may believe he's completely impassive, but he writhes in rage. Indifferent? He's desperately in love. You're not impressed by his icy control? It took him years to get like this! He used to hold ice cubes over his forehead in the bathroom when he was a child, to get just the right cold, blank stare.

The Scorpster expects you to live up to your word, your promise, your life mission, and your divine purpose. His standards for human behavior exceed those of Miss Manners, Dear Abby, and Mother Teresa. Does Scorpio have faith in the human race? Nope. That's your job—to live up to his towering moral demands and restore his belief in human goodness. And you thought you were just falling in love.

When Scorpio himself falls in love, he may turn cold, paranoid, and uncommunicative. In fact, he may battle you to the death for having the gall to capture his heart. Once he's romantically corrupted, however, he wastes no time in taking possession. Of you. This means you stop all that stupid socializing and cease looking at other men. (Hard to do if you work, since your male colleagues will wonder why you're suddenly staring at the floor.) It also means you give in to Scorpio on all possible occasions, since he does not relish being crossed in any way.

Furthermore, while he photocopies your diary for further study, you learn nothing he does not want you to know—such as where he was born, who his best friend is, or the name of his dog. If you're the submissive type who wonders what life was like as the concubine of a pharaoh, puzzle no further.

Do you yearn for sweet nothings whispered in your ear? Do you crave compliments in the boudoir? Poetry in the moonlight? Sorry, pal. Scorpio does not stoop to low and vulgar sentiment—spoken aloud, no less—while he's performing the horizontal mambo. Best you appreciate his mysterious, speechless self. Besides, the depth of his gaze should be enough for you.

## * The Bad Stuff

Beware of a man who tells you he has a sense of humor.

Fasten your seatbelts! *The ego has landed!* Is he wiser than Buddha? Smarter than Einstein? Just ask—Scorp never holds back when it comes to discussing his genius. If you look closely, you can see a big, grey balloon following him wherever he goes. This is his ego, which is too large to be contained in one mere personality. So it tags along behind him, frightening people. If you want to spend your life with this man, consider having rose-colored contacts surgically implanted.

He's not really into revenge. The Scorpion just needs to teach spiritual lessons to the rest of us—and his lessons make the Mafia look like Peter Rabbit. Have you flirted with another man? The Scorpster is peeved. And you are dead. You, your reputation, your dog's reputation, your emotional health, your career track, your status in the neighborhood—these are all, each and every one of them, destroyed. Ravaged. Ruined. And he's just peeved! Think what he can do when he's really annoyed.

The Scorpster is into pain—other people's. If the enemy does not writhe in anguish, he is not fulfilled. Let's try another psychic torpedo. Unlike other signs, Scorpio attacks for fun and profit. There's the Sneak Attack (his favorite), the Just-Because Attack (he's bored), the Sunday-Breakfast Attack (just when you thought it was safe to use egg substitute), the Dinner-With-Inlaws Attack (you can run, but you cannot hide), and the You-Dared-To-Contradict-Him Attack (be afraid; be very afraid).

Scorpio is not into apologies. Apology? Isn't that a Greek dish? Neither is he humbly grateful. He belongs to the human race—anything more humbling than that he could not possibly envision. And grateful? He should have received a medal for being born. It's called "entitlement," and Scorpio has it in spades. The world owes him, and it had better pay up. Or someone will be very, very sorry.

Never give him a surprise party. Never. It will take you six weeks to get everyone there on time, hiding in the kitchen, with a big cake waiting in the wings. In he will walk, as everyone yells "Surprise!" Is he surprised? Is he pleased? Is he dead? How can you tell? With his usual detached, emotionless expression, the

Scorpster greets each guest as if he were teaching a class in accounting. Quietly, he asks if you're out of toothpaste. Quietly, he departs to the bathroom to brush his teeth, because that's what he always does when he gets home. Let everyone else party til they drop. He of the Detached, Unruffled Soul will graciously consent to be pleased, inside, where no one can tell. Drop the word "surprise" from your vocabulary. You'll save on therapy bills.

He's not really looking for a trophy wife, he'll be satisfied as long as every other man in the Western Hemisphere wants you, too. Once again, it's about p-o-w-e-r. He loves you for yourself alone, and he also loves you for what you can do for his ego. He is his ego, so feel honored that he has chosen you to stroke it. So to speak.

## ✳ How Scorpio Likes His Women

You are sensual, perceptive, and you have an astute intelligence which you do not need to put on parade. You don't compete with men; you complement them. This is good, because he competes with himself and doesn't need any interference. You understand the deep value of interdependence, and you are unafraid to lean, when leaning is called for. You refuse to conform. You do things your way, and if your way is quirky and private, so much the better.

And finally, you have what they used to call "character." There are limits. There are things with which you will not put up. And there are values for which you stand, which makes him love and admire you with all the depth of his soul.

## ✳ What the Scorpion Sees When He Looks at You

You are Eve. Your fabulous femininity defies description. Your eyes hold a thousand secrets.

Merely sipping your coffee is an act of mystery. You revel in the difference between men and women, and your intellect is not threatened by gender wars. You adore the multiple roles men can play in your life, and you let them know it.

Although males have been known to fall at your feet in droves, you have eyes only for your true love. You look fabulous in long skirts, woven shawls, and cotton dresses, as well as heels, silk stockings, and little-nothing slips. You wear clothes that cling—in all the right places. Your hair gleams with care; your eyes are soft and clear. You are a magnificent listener. You love to laugh.

## ✶ What Turns Him On

Power. Mystery. Subtlety. To be overpowered by mystery, subtly. To penetrate your mystery, to mesmerize you with his power—you get the idea. But you know things about the human heart and mind that he does not. And as you stare right back at him, you smile, slightly, in acknowledgement of the stratagems he's devised to capture your interest. You see them all. They amuse you. But you're after deeper things.

Is sex all there is between a man and a woman? You think not. There are untold mysteries to be solved, uncharted countries of flesh and spirit to be uncovered. Have you found a man who can possess your soul? Perhaps. Perhaps not yet. You give nothing away. . . .

## ✶ What Rules the Scorpion

Pride, God and Gonads. You should be able to tell the difference, since he never can. The Scorpster's burning intensity is actually spiritual, although it

manifests itself in the appetites. Remember this as
he's coming on to you with that *Terminator* glaze in
his eyes. It won't help, but you'll feel part of a
larger purpose.

## THE CHASE

### * His Secret Paradox

He despises people who need people, and how
churlish of Fate that he himself should fall into that
category. He scorns emotional vulnerability, but
has a desperately susceptible heart. He thus despises and scorns parts of himself. The Scorpster
doesn't make it easy. He'd prefer that you believe
his Lonesome-Cowboy act, but what he'd really
like is to be safe and cozy by the fire, all wrapped
up with his sweetheart in his arms. Only when he
realizes that the ability to be vulnerable is strength,
not weakness, will he begin to resolve his many
contradictions.

### * How to Bewitch Scorpio

You have hypnotized him with your undivided attention. You thoughtfully concentrate on his every
word. You take him very, *very* seriously. You ask
for suggestions on subjects of mutual interest.
Would he instruct you? So much the better. And
you, oh Womanly One, can communicate with so
much more than words! Your eyes, your mouth,
your very skin speak languages that only he can
fathom. No one could ever call you aggressive, so
how did you manage to pervade his very soul
when he wasn't looking? It wasn't what you said.
It was nothing overt. But he finds himself—my

God! possessed!—in ways he can't begin to describe. *How did you do it???* Seeking the answer to this will drive him crazy and keep him riveted for years to come.

## ✳ Don't . . .

Snoop, if you value your life. When he turns his death-ray stare on you, ask if he uses a dandruff shampoo. Point out his faults (what faults?). Read comic books in bed. Read them aloud. Serve leftover anchovy pizza for dinner. Tell him assault fantasies are so '50s. Giggle when he broods. Tell him you love to laugh in bed. When he turns his tragic, haunted face toward yours, tell him he has enlarged pores.

## ✳ Whom He Likes to Bed

Do not mistake his nature. Except in the worst escapist moods, the Scorpster is never satisfied with a back-door quickie. What's he really after? Oh, the Mystery of Life will do. He seeks to penetrate the secrets of the divine through ecstatic physical union. His sheer intensity would set the sheets on fire. And that place where the pleasure is so intense it is almost unbearable—ah, now there's an affair to remember! Are you looking for a night you'll never forget? You are provocative. You are intense. You seek the unknown frontiers of the flesh. Have you ever had so many orgasms that you passed out? No, but tonight you will. . . .

## ✳ Whom He Likes to Wed

A woman with "bottom," as the English used to say. A woman of exceptional character, who can withstand the tumultuous Scorpion theatrics. She who will see the trembling sensitivity beneath the sly—nay, brutal—exterior. She who remains cool as he desperately tries to avoid falling in love with her. A woman who can read minds at 500 yards. Who can amuse him in an intellectual game, yet who longs to feel vanquished by his staggering male power. A woman who knows how to nurture without extinguishing the all-important sexual flame. A practical soul who comprehends the value of the long haul, maritally speaking, and joyfully looks forward to her fiftieth wedding anniversary. And, finally, a woman who doesn't mind his drawerful of personal secrets, which he needs like other people need food and water.

## * What He's Secretly Afraid Of

Those tiny holes near his eyes are tear ducts, used by most humans to release softer feelings. Women prefer lighthearted lovers. There is no God. Someday he might have an emotional need. It's not soul; it's depression. The joke's on him. Everyone's snickering. That little motor in his chest is a heart, not a decoding machine. People who need people are luckier. Failure is an important part of success. He'd make a great clown. Control freaks have inferior orgasms. He's a blonde at heart.

## * When to Say Yes

The "yes" has to be there, in the air, from the beginning. He likes a challenge, but the challenge should be how to make you his, not do you want him in the first place. You will know when to say yes, because you will be overpowered by an all-encompassing male force that you cannot resist.

Your meek little "yes" will be lost in the gale force of his desire.

What's more important with Scorpio, and what will thrill him beyond words, is your total, complete surrender—when you say yes with your heart, your mind, and your soul. There is nothing left. He, the hurricane. You, the trembling banana leaf. You get the idea.

## THE COUP DE GRACE

### * His Sexual Secrets and Desires

Scorpio is synonymous with sex. Scorpio seeks passion: mental, emotional, and spiritual. But don't be intimidated. Concentrate on some serious sex and leave the Holy Grail to him.

Let there be water. If you don't live near the sea, get one of those sound machines that makes distant wave noises. Scorpio doesn't need frilly sheets and pink candles; we are not into *Rebecca of Sunnybrook Farm* here. Have you always yearned to be taken on the floor of a barn? How about the back of a truck? This man is sexual first, sensual second. It's about tension, timing, power, and explosion. It's about edge.

He likes extremes of pleasure. He likes that exquisite pleasure/pain threshold. So you're not going to violate anything—you're just going to heighten his perception a little. You're on the floor. There is chilled Chablis. There are apples, pears, and chocolate. There is a small bottle of edible oil, softly scented with oranges. The floor is comfortable, but not a featherbed. It might even have a certain roughness to it. This is sex, not a massage.

The lights are low; the room is utterly, completely private. There is distant, hypnotic music.

Feed him a chocolate while you pour a few drops of oil on your fingers. Let a few drops fall on him. Start with his nipples, which you caress and pinch until they are stiff little soldiers. Now slowly lick his nipples clean. Then massage his stomach, licking it off after you're done. This will give him an idea of the future. Use more oil and tease your fingers in between his balls and his anus, massaging that part of him until he is slick and wet. Softly finger his anus with one slippery hand, while you massage his balls with the other. Slowly. Slowly.

Let a few drops of oil fall on his crotch. Now move your fingers lightly, reverently, up his penis, and play with the little hole at the top. Slide back down. Massage him with long, slow strokes until he is stiff and slick and glistening. Now bend down and begin to lick. Lick his balls, lightly at first, little cat licks. Hold them in your mouth as you tongue him. When he is swollen and hard, move your tongue up to his penis. Lick him from the bottom to the tip in long, slow, hard strokes.

Now stop for a second and take a small, hand-held vibrator, and stroke it between his ass and his balls. Continue to lick him as you would lick an ice cream cone, with round, wide strokes. Bring him just to the point of orgasm; then stop.

Take a sip of wine. Take your time. Let him wait. Before you take him in your mouth again, place the vibrator on the delicate skin right in front of his anus, and hold it there. Take him in your mouth and begin to massage him with your tongue. Keep the vibrator pressed close to the skin. As he starts to climax, continue to softly massage him with your mouth, move the virbator down his anus, and turn it up to "high."

You may have to revive him with a splash of cold water after this.

### * Shhh . . .

Try having sex anywhere. A broom closet. The subway. The kitchen floor. An empty swimming pool. A filled swimming pool. Sand dunes. Garage floors. Alleyways. Cornfields. Graveyards. And that's just the first week.

## AFTERGLOW: WHAT YOU NEED TO KNOW

### * What Scorpio Likes Better than Sex

Control. As in unlimited personal power. The problem with power, however, is that no one ever gives it to you—you have to take it. Thus, Scorpio's life ambition is to grab as much power as he can possibly can, from every conceivable source. Introduce him to the mysterious joys of shared command. It'll knock his spiritual socks off.

### * Will He Marry His Best Lover or Best Friend?

The Scorpion longs to give himself completely in love—no small task—and for that he needs the most singularly special woman in the world. She transcends all categories of friend and lover, to him. Once he has found her, he will stop at nothing to make her his.

P.S.—She'll be no slouch in the boudoir, either.

## ✳ What He Wants from You

Stimulation! Sexual, emotional, and intellectual. Total focus on him and his needs. Your willing compliance with his every whim (we didn't say he should have it, just that he wants it). Constant affection, freely given at all times, but especially in private. A shared solitude. Scorpio is into the idea of service—yours. Do you have just a touch of the secret slave about you? All the better to arouse his passions. What he dearly longs for, however, but can't express, is a little right-brained enchantment and mystery in his controlled, analyzed life. Give it to him and watch him glow.

## ✳ What He Needs From You

Certainty. The assurance that you are on his side, totally and completely, and that you will never be on anyone else's. He also needs you to acknowledge his vast reserves of strength, loyalty and power, and to hold them in your heart, where he can see his best qualities reflected should he happen to hit a dark moment. Never, ever taper off the affection. More than anything, Scorpio needs a fortress of privacy where it's safe for him to reveal his feelings, which frighten him to death.

## ✳ What He Won't Give up For You

Scorpio will never give up his need to penetrate the mysteries: animal, mineral, human, or divine. Nor will he give up his alien-in-disguise persona, his need to play with other people's heads, or his yen for serious solitude. Or his rage to possess you, his drive to succeed, his eternal game-playing, his zero-sum cool. In fact, with one or two notable exceptions, the

Scorpster does not give up. He allows you to accommodate yourself to him. But he's cool about it.

## * What He Will Give up For You

He will unequivocally give up all hints of other women. The Scorpion is obsessively loyal; it's one of his most beautiful gifts to you. If he's well loved, he may give up the more pretentious aspects of his brooding, I-Am-An-Island act. But that's it. Everything else stays. Giving up sounds too much like surrender, which is too close to defeat, which gives all Scorpions cardiac arrest.

## * How to Make Him Fall in Love With You, Really

Falling in love means his Lone Ranger image has to bite the dust, and no cell in Scorpio's body willingly bites the dust. He's not really cold, remote and mean. He's hot, out of control, and frighteningly defensive. If you pay very close attention, you will begin to see what others can't. Trust him. Believe that he yearns for a great love, that he has an impossible time exposing his heart, and that he's so emotional it terrifies him. Scorpio is a cactus tree. You don't believe that spiny plant can put forth gorgeous blossoms? Believe. Give him your absolute loyalty and your absolute faith, wrap him in waves of warmth and comfort, and he will begin to bloom in miraculous ways that will capture your heart forever.

## * Make It Forever

Have you ever touched anything so hot it felt cold? That's Scorpio in a nutshell. Once you've proved your loyalty to him beyond doubt, let him know how much you admire his sterling qualities. Some achieve greatness, and some have greatness thrust upon them. Thrust some greatness upon your Scorpio, since he will live up to your loftiest expectations and then some. Let him know that control is a synonym for fear, and where there is great love, there is no room for fear. Underneath his super-solitude act is a little boy who's afraid of being abandoned. Love him with all your heart and soul, hold nothing back, and he will reward you with a devotion that will take your breath away.

## CRUCIAL MINUTIAE

### ✳ What to Feed Scorpio

The Scorpion loves to indulge in food, drink, and other mysterious substances. Therefore, feed him lavish, sensual food that stimulates more than one appetite at once. Think finger food—long slices of juicy melon for breakfast, with fresh-ground coffee and little breast-shaped sweet rolls, will revive him after a night of excess. For a snack, find the ripest, juiciest peaches available; serve with chilled chardonnay, and a smear of overripe Brie on black raisin bread. Anything that's luscious, round, and can be sucked on will do nicely, such as ripe pears, black olives, or dark chocolate truffles. And don't neglect his drinking pleasure! Offer him a deep, smoky burgundy or merlot with wild game for dinner, and hand him a snifter of brandy by the fire. Deep, dark flavors such as a cabernet, espresso, or brandy-spiced hot chocolate will soon have him staring at you under that black magic moon.

## * How to Take Care of Your Scorpion

Subtly. The Scorpion does not take kindly to being told what to do. Too much fussing is what his mother used to do, and you are not his mother. However, he needs care just as much as the rest of us, if not more, since he burns the candle at both ends, in the middle, and up and down the sides. Go to the gym with him and sign up for a weight-lifting class, or kickboxing or karate. Getting that explosive energy flowing out of his system will do wonders for the Scorpster's health and well-being. Swimming will definitely help him cool down and rebalance his energies, and so will long hikes. Fly a kite together. It's one of those lighthearted experiences that he can load with deep meaning. Introduce him to walking meditation, which will slow him down and focus him in the present. And, finally, kidnap him for a weekend by the sea, with only the waves, the gulls, and you.

## * For His Birthday

Travel! Scorpio likes mysteries, likes to explore, likes to uncover secrets. Surprise him with one of those archeological travel trips where not only do you get to climb over the ruins together; you get to participate in an actual dig.

All traveled out? Find a church with an ancient graveyard where you can both read the headstones. See if you can uncover any family secrets. Send him to a good astrologer or psychic—he'll protest, but he'll be secretly fascinated. Give him a subscription to a good science magazine, or a journal of Eastern religion. For his birthday, have a mystery party (buy a mystery game) where he's the detective and one of your friends is the murderer. He'll object, of course, but he'll have more fun than he'd ever admit to.

# sagittarius

## NOVEMBER 23 - DECEMBER 21

### BEST LOVE MATCHES

Sagittarius & Aries
Sagittarius & Leo
Sagittarius & Libra
Sagittarius & Aquarius

He's a first-class wit with a vagabond charm. He's the center of the in-crowd, and he's so much fun he's positively indecent. He's Sagittarius, the Centaur.

## FAMOUS SAGITTARIANS

Mark Twain, Walt Disney, John F. Kennedy, Jr., Brad Pitt, Steven Spielberg, Jim Morrison, Gianni Versace, Kenneth Branagh, Larry Bird, Woody Allen

## I AM

Impossibly charmed by you. Another drink? Do you come here often? What's your sign? Is there a pickup cliché I've missed? Hi. If you smile I'll put a stop to the rumor that our host paid you to come here tonight and drive all the men to distraction. Thank you! You have a dazzling smile.

Oops! Oh, God. Spilling a drink down your arm is not my standard bait. God, I'm sorry! How's your dress? If you'll take it off, I'll have it cleaned for you. I mean, not now. I mean, send me the bill. It was that damn carpet's fault. They shouldn't make carpets with lumps in them—what's hiding under there? A dead canary? You're being awfully nice about this. Stress becomes you.

You have the most gorgeous eyes I've ever seen. Is that your real color, or are those contacts? Tell you what. It's a full moon tonight, and you can see Orion's belt if you're standing clear in a meadow. I've got an old sweat suit in my trunk; why not put it on and come with me? You don't look overly slender—it ought to fit. The great pyramid in Egypt was built in a direct line to Orion's belt, so the soul of the pharaoh could fly straight to the stars. Let me show you! Let's go!

By the way, I'm biking through Tibet next month; want to come along? Thank God I'm brilliant at my job—they let me travel a lot. I could be making a lot more dough in another office, but anyone who works solely for money is wasting his time on earth.

You don't mind that I said you weren't overly slender, do you? Hey! It's much healthier to carry a few extra pounds! You look built for babies! Not that you'd be having mine. Anyway, I'm constitutionally incapable of lying. The truth is the most interesting thing we have to work with, and I seek the truth at every possible opportunity—philosophical, emotional and sexual.

I'm looking to get enraptured, not entrapped. I trust you feel the same. Although sometimes I dream of a great love—she who would travel down the Yangtze with me and make love all during the monsoon rains. But I doubt she exists. Frankly, I view marriage with a kind of horror. Why on earth would someone eat hamburger every night for the rest of his life when he could have steak, pizza, Kung Pao, escargot, moussaka—you take my meaning.

The "now" is all we have. This moment, this night. I cannot live for some superficial future that doesn't exist. But you still have the most gorgeous eyes I've ever seen. Hey! Do you samba? Shall we dance?

## YOU ARE

Absolutely irresistible. You have to be, because I am the world's champion resister. Are you beautiful? In the eyes of the beholder, namely me, you are breathtaking. But that half-assed compliment wasn't good enough for you, was it? Since you are also vain (sorry, Truth is my thing), and you invest enough in your looks to make sure heads will turn. And if heads don't turn, heads will roll, n'est-ce pas? You're quite imperious when in the mood, my dear.

You are also one impetuous, tempestuous dame. What I adore about you is that you are up for anything—ice swimming, hot-air ballooning, a month in the country, a year in China. Your life force could power a small city all night, which is perfect, because I could not bear an unenthusiastic woman. You love to laugh—laughter is more romantic than roses to you. Although roses had better show up on February fourteenth or major hell will break loose. Jokes, even practical jokes, don't faze you, fortunately for both of us, since I can't help myself.

You are passion personified. You would stay up all night just to fight with me. Or to make love til dawn. Or to watch the stars glitter and grow pale because you've never seen the dawn in Cannes before. You have a career because it helps focus your extraordinary energy and ambition, and your aggressiveness doesn't disturb me; it turns me on. Although it certainly disturbs lesser, fainthearted souls.

Merely washing dishes with you is a blast—not that we do a lot of that—and you've been known to throw one or two just to make a point. You are a beautiful, intense, driven soul who champions the underdog at great cost to yourself, if necessary. Especially if necessary. You love telling people what to do, and the trouble is, you're so good at it. You refuse to be bored, even at the risk of offending people. But you offend them so graciously.

You not only make love; you make magic. Yet you are canny enough to take a look at me and love me anyway, with your whole generous, hotheaded soul, because your wisdom tells you that that is the only way to love. You are someone I secretly dreamed of but never thought I'd find—my intellectual equal, my road warrior, my own dear love.

## HOW TO DRIVE ME WILD

Don't make it easy. Please, please don't make it easy. You look impossible to achieve—I love that. You also look like you know what to do when we get there. I like that even better. So talk to me. Keep it up for hours, for several evenings, in fact. Let me know with your eyes what you're going to do to me when we meet in the dark. But don't give in too soon. The look, the glance, the hint, the dance—this is what I live for! Romance is adventure. And if it isn't, it should be.

Make me come after you. Way after. But don't lead me on—I hate that, and I'll call you on it in front of all your friends. Make me laugh. Let me know just how difficult it is to capture your interest. A glass of wine? Another dance, just the two of us? Here? Alone? I'm fond of that dress; all dresses should be designed for maximum leg exposure. But fond as I am, I think it should come off right about now. Take it off in time to the music. Don't stop dancing. I like that bra; I like the way it shows off your nipples. Don't stop dancing. Are those French-cut panty hose? Marvelous. The better to see you, my dear.

I want you to unbutton my shirt; take it off, but don't stop dancing. Now take off my pants. Put your hand on me, you know where, and move it in time to the music, to the dance. By the way, do you have a vibrator? I want to use it on you, but not now—later. Now kiss me. Keep massaging me. Have you ever done this before? Marvelous! This will be your first dancing lesson.

I want to see your desire. Show me how wet you are. Show me you want me. Now arch yourself back while I slide inside you. Wrap your legs around me; I can hold you. Keep dancing. That's the important part, darling. Keep dancing. You don't think I can keep dancing while I'm inside you? Oh, ye of little faith! Of course, we may have to lean against the wall right about now. Your nakedness is driving me crazy, you know. No! Don't stop dancing. Kiss me, and don't stop moving like that. Kiss me, and move against me, that's right, now, against the wall. Kiss me. You're suspiciously good at this. Kiss me again . . . and don't stop.

## CONFIDENTIALLY YOURS

### ✳ What He Won't Tell You

He's got you under his skin . . . and skin-deep is just about how far you'll get with Sag. He's a will-o'-the-wisp who's in love with you because, well, you're there! If you're not there, he'll make do nicely with the blonde next door, the redhead across the hall, or the brunette downstairs.

Sagittarius is extremely entertaining and extremely well liked. Don't be taken in by the hopelessly charming routine, however. Mr. Popular keeps close tabs on his personal charisma. Are his ratings slipping? Pump up the volume! Did someone yawn? Crank up the charm! Some are born charismatic and some achieve charisma by working their little butts off. Sag is of the latter category. Enjoy his performance. It took him years to get this smooth.

Sag is a world-class vagabond who keeps a packed knapsack handy in case an adventure thrusts itself upon him. An adventure, however, is anything that gets him out of the house, such as checking out the Häagen Dazs flavors at the local 7–Eleven. Don't be surprised if he tells you he's going out for a quart of milk and reappears six months later, with a brazen grin. Will you take him in? You will, you hussy, because his charm is lethal and you're positively hypnotized by his total lack of shame.

You observe he's a little clumsy. Spilling a drink

down your arm is just the tip of the Sagittarian iceberg. Stepping on your feet while dancing, pulling your hair when making out, kneeling on your elbow during 69—expect this and more from Mr. Sag as he tries to maintain his romantic cool. Don't be fooled, however, into labeling him an endearing, puppyish naïf. He is nothing of the sort. He is merely a dangerously charming libertine with two left feet. Give him ballet lessons for his birthday or stock up on Vitamin C for all those bruises in your future.

You note he refers to women as steak, pizza, Kung Pao, and escargot. To Mr. Sag, women are the delectable, ever-changing smorgasbord to which life treats him, free of charge. Is it Tuesday? This must be Susan. To his credit, Sag always finds what's-her-name absolutely mesmerizing. Even more mesmerizing is the fact that women these days conveniently return to their own self-reliant lives after a *nuit d'amour*. How perfect can you get?

If you crave long nights of intensely passionate, emotional lovemaking, *escaaaape nowwwwwwwwww!* Love is like badminton to Sagittarius. It's light as a feather, you don't break a sweat, and you can play in the most elegant clothes. So what if you lose? Just float the little birdie over the net and start in again. In general, Sag does not:

1. carry a torch
2. recite poetry under your window, unless it's naughty and it rhymes
3. try to possess your soul (soul? you have one?)
4. get possessive
5. fall in fierce-and-dramatic love

So if you're looking for lasting love, you may have to keep looking. If you're looking for merriment, jest, and fine sport, look no further. Of course, you may be that exceedingly rare woman who can bring out both in Sag. Are you? Then bravo! You've found your man.

## \* The Bad Stuff

He is dedicated to life, puberty, and the pursuit of his penis.

Is he critiquing your makeup? Your outfit? Your hair? Lucky you! He's fallen in love! Like Leo, Sag fancies himself a molder of female flesh. Not only do you get a lover; you get a personal trainer, coach, and managing director—free! Tell him to back off, but tell him politely, you ungrateful little lump of clay.

Birds do it, bees do it, and so does Sag, on every possible occasion. Like the bee, Sag flits from female to female, democratically meting out his favors. Here a little pollen, there a little dew. How lucky for the female race that he declines to hoard himself! How fortunate that hundreds, perhaps thousands, of women will get to sample his charms! Marriage? Pfft! Not while there's a woman alive who needs his services. Heroically, he will plow on, planting his tribute to womankind wherever he may roam—a kind of Bedroom Johnny Appleseed.

Morals? Sag's theme song is "Call Me Irresponsible." He has no morals. Not in the bedroom, that is. He certainly couldn't think of anything less inviting than ethical considerations mucking up his sex life. We're all adults here, right? We all know who, er, what we're getting into. He thought so.

Sex is the parade. Morals are rain. End of story.

On the other hand, truth to Sag is a spiritual quest. Remember this as he observes in front of forty people that you look stuffed into your pants and really ought to leave that piece of pizza for someone with more self-control. He's only being supportive. You don't want people calling you "chunko" behind your back, do you? He's only trying to help. You really do need to lose a little weight. See? His motives are pure. His purpose is high. And his ass is grass—if you have the self-respect you were born with.

Unfortunately, while the truthful Sagittarius is painful, the tactful Sagittarius is much worse. Have foot in mouth, will travel. If you're wearing sunscreen, he'll cheer you up by remarking that your wrinkles couldn't possibly get any worse, so why bother. Many brave souls flinch when they see him trying to maneuver a compliment out of his mouth. However, the Heavenly Truthteller can clam up completely when it comes to his personal romantic affairs. Don't even bother to ask. Details? He'll grin like the Cheshire Cat. And then he'll disappear.

He says he loves the chase. This means he will spend 50 hours getting you to bed and .50 minutes keeping you there. Ready and waiting? Good! This shouldn't take more than a minute. It's not that Sag is a quick draw in the bedroom—it's just that he likes to get it over with while his clothes are still warm. That way he'll be dressed and ready for the next encounter.

Can you spell *cad*? Romantically speaking, Sag will not join any club that would have him as a member. This means that if a woman is perverted enough to fall deeply in love with him, he certainly wouldn't want anything to do with her. How low can she go? Pretty low, if she yearns for him. He, personally, would not stoop to falling in love with anyone as fickle and depraved as himself. He pities the poor damsel who does. Usually from afar.

To Sag, the hunt is all. Chasing a rabbit is always more fun than catching it, he feels. Once you've caught your prey, there's disposal of the body, always a messy task. It's the same with women. What to do with them once their allure has worn off? Gosh! Girls! You can't live with 'em, you can't sell 'em for their fur! What's a fun-loving boy to do?

## ∗ How Sagittarius Likes His Women

Non-possessive. Un-clinging. Independent. You are equally at home on safari, white-water rafting, or nightclub hopping. You turn life and love into one huge adventure. Witty and erudite, you see no reason why great conversation and a glass of champagne can't go hand in hand with tiger hunting. (You will photograph the tigers, not shoot them. You are a conservationist at heart.)

Problems are trifles to you, to be disposed of swiftly lest they interfere with your unbridled lust for life. A great talker and an equally great listener, you are intellectually curious. You are also a world-class flirt. Men are game—fair game or unfair, it matters not. Your most trivial glance entices in that maddening, black-magic way. You are up for anything—anything at all—and you demand that your lover live up to your challenge.

## ∗ What Sag Sees When He Looks At You

Your eyes are alight with laughter and sanity. You are always ready to be amused, and you have a generosity that enjoys humor wherever you may find it. Your hair is a gorgeous, sensuous mane, whether it's one or twenty inches long. You take exquisite care of yourself; you enjoy being pampered, and if no one else is around, you'll do it yourself. Your are strong, emotionally and physically, and equally at home in jeans or Versace. In fact, you look like a million dollars at all times, even if you're living on rice cakes and raisins.

You have a regal, dynamic air about you that stops traffic at fifty paces, and a way of commanding any room you are in. Although you positively exude sex, your slightly aloof posture warns that you were not made for the common man, but for that rare soul who can capture your intellect, your heart, and all other vital parts of your anatomy.

## ✴ What Turns Him On

Wit. Cleverness. Repartee. If you aren't strong in these areas, listen to him and laugh a lot. He doesn't like to feel that he's "getting into anything," particularly at the moment when he's getting into you. So be sure he knows that you're fond of adventure—romantic, sexual, or otherwise—for its own sake.

You don't have a marriage contract hidden in your bra, and, in fact, you're not even looking. What? Give up your adventurous, fascinating life to settle down with the same old same-old? You hope he's not suggesting this! You need to be entertained; you need wide open spaces; you haven't been to Bali yet! And while you're on the subject, just how amusing is he? So many men, so little time, sigh. . . .

## ✳ What Rules Sag

Wanderlust. Wandering all over the map and lusting at all possible times. Lusting after the Truth and wandering around in search of it. Wandering in search of lust. Lusting while wandering.

# THE CHASE

## ✳ His Secret Paradox

Mr. Sag wants to be unfettered, unchained, and free. But he also yearns to be understood by the perfect woman who will positively not try to change him, but love him as he is. He knows he's impossible, so he figures that loving him is impossible, too. It's not, of course, but Sag fights falling in love, so he makes it all the harder to achieve harmony with his beloved. Keep still and vibe him out until he keels over from the sheer unthreatening warmth of your presence. Teach him that dreams can be real.

## ✳ How to Bewitch Sagittarius

Listen to him. He's fascinating. Conversation to Sag is like a Cole Porter song—the wittier and more sophisticated, the better he likes it. And he's heavily into pursuit. This means—challenge!! He wants to come after you; he wants it to be a little difficult; he wants to wrest you away from the arms of dozens of lesser men by the sheer brilliance of his charm and wit. So make sure you're worth the game. If you're a little aggressive, so much the better—Sag doesn't like a clinging vine.

Furthermore, as long as there's the thrill of the

chase or the tang of a mystery to be solved, he's off and running, so make sure you're in tow. Above all, Sag likes to have fun, whether it's a drive-in movie or a lecture on metaphysical entropy. So keep things light, fast-paced, and witty, and he will keep in close and fascinated pursuit.

### * Don't . . .

Ask him to repeat the punch line. Tell him you don't get it. Tell him you have to be in bed by ten. Refuse to sleep with him until he puts the Airedale in the other room. Refuse to eat with him until he puts the Airedale's dish on the floor. Feel sorry for yourself. Nag. Make polite requests. Worry. Tell him you get seasick. Suggest that he's fibbing.

### * Who He Likes to Bed

Who doesn't he? But if he has to choose, Sag prefers amusing, adventuresome types to whom love is a lemon souffle—a froth of sugar and air that feels wonderful going down, but won't stick to your ribs in the morning. He likes his women sophisticated and skilled, but don't despair if you're the country-mouse type. He also loves to teach.

Mr. Sag's specialty, however, is appealing to your maternal instincts. He's got the hopelessly-charming-bumbling-male act down pat. Do you just want to kidnap him and take care of him? He's got you right where he wants you! But go ahead. You'll have a ball.

### * Who He Likes to Wed

Wed??? As in lock????? Sag is one of those signs who usually doesn't ripen into husbandom until the late third or fourth decade. If you know a young and immature Sag and you're dying to be married, get a sheepdog instead. They're loyal, faithful, dedicated, and only have (weak) eyes for you. Train yourself to expect this from a man.

If you still want your Sag, be a bold, impetuous spirit who's not heavily into domestica. You enjoy him for his marvelous, complex mind, and you grant him the same freedom and solitude you grant yourself. You demand excitement and affection from your lover, and you give equal measure in return.

## ✳ What He's Secretly Afraid Of

It's not wanderlust; it's escapism. That egg timer by the bed is for his orgasm. No one wants to hear the truth, bald or otherwise. Clumsy men make clumsy lovers. Bringing out a woman's maternal instinct does not drive her insane with lust. Domestic bliss is fun. Children can be unexpectedly fulfilling. If he falls asleep, he'll miss something.

## ✳ When to Say Yes

Sexually? Lead him on a merry chase; he'll adore you for it. Say yes when you've driven him insane with desire, having teased and flirted your way around the mulberry bush enough times to make him dizzy. Marriage-wise? If he asks you, stare at him blankly and say, "Marriage? Would it tie me down?" This deeply reassures Sag that he has chosen the right woman.

# THE COUP DE GRACE

### ✴ His Sexual Secrets and Desires

The Centaur is a thrill-seeker, and he believes fun's no good unless it's *really* fun. While Sag would enjoy an erotic encounter while parachuting over the Mojave during a sandstorm, don't ignore the entertainment value of your own backyard.

Invite him to a very unusual picnic. You're wearing stockings. They're black and seamed. They're held up by a little-nothing black lace garter. You're wearing the kind of heels that give you miles and miles of leg. This is good, since you're also wearing a long, diaphanous skirt that's slit up to here, the better to show off your legs, and a silken top that invites further research.

You hand him champagne and invite him outside into the secluded garden. There is a cloth on the grass, and candles, and many pillows. Also music, something light and sophisticated. There are baskets of nibbly things such as grapes, cheese straws, olives, and fingers of dark chocolate.

Tell him you'd like to dance. While you're foxtrotting on the grass, ask him if he'd like to play strip poker. Have him sit down on the opposite side of the blanket. Neither of you can touch each other or cross the blanket until someone wins. The winner takes the loser as a slave for the rest of the night. Pour a little more champagne. Deal the cards.

The first time you lose, take off your blouse. Toss it lightly onto the blanket, over near him. Are you a little warm? Take an ice cube and rub it lightly up and down your chest as you play. The fourth time you lose, reach up and take off your black silk garter. Toss it lightly near his lap.

Mention casually that you've never be able to find your G-spot. No man has ever been skilled enough to stimulate it for you. You wonder where it is. How you wish you could climax like that. You've heard that finger exploration should come first, with further penetration later.

The final hand arrives. You are wearing nothing but lipstick and black silk panties. When you lose this hand, as you inevitably must, tell him that if he wants you to remove your panties, he has to take them off with his teeth. No hands.

### ✳ Shhh . . .

Meet him for a drink at a conservative bar. Wear nothing but a trenchcoat and expensive shoes.

## AFTERGLOW: WHAT YOU NEED TO KNOW

### ✳ What Sag Likes Better Than Sex

A-roving we will go! A-roving we will go! Heigh-ho the merry-o! A-roving we will go! Is there a plane to Casablanca tonight? A slow boat to Fiji? He's outta here!

### ✳ Will He Marry His Best Lover Or Best Friend?

He won't, ah, marry until some impossibly clever female tricks him into realizing he's really far better off as a team. And she will be a fabulous companion (read "friend") who has an exciting, sparkling sex drive to match his own.

### ✳ What He Wants From You

Fun! Amusement! Daring! Adventure! Exploration! Personal Guided Tours! The ideal Sag girlfriend sounds like the perfect travel brochure. Furthermore, you don't cost much in the way of emotional baggage, and you bring your own toothbrush. He's a thrill-seeker; he's endlessly curious; everything's sharper and funnier when he's around. Including you.

## ✱ What He Needs From You

Understanding. All men are unique, but Sag is really unique. Like Aquarius, he's a thinker and a dreamer, but unlike Aquarius, he's got a warm heart. Like Leo, he's wise and free with his opinions, but unlike Leo, he has no desire to possess the air you breathe. A street-smart idealist and an affectionate freedom-lover, Sag needs your perception and tolerance, two qualities he will give you in spades. And last, he needs you to carry his dream for him. Whatever his vision, it will be lofty and filled with ambitious purpose, so carry it deep in your heart where you believe in him totally and love him completely.

## ✱ What He Won't Give Up For You

In one corner of his soul, there will always be a candle burning on the bachelor altar. He loves you because, fortunately, you understand this.

## ✱ What He Will Give Up For You

If you're really lucky, and the moon is right, and he's actually talking himself into the M-word, he will give up his fetishistic obsession with the Faerie Queen, his ideal love who will enchant him endlessly for the rest of his days. This nonexistent creature has provided him with the perfect escape clause in his many romances. If he truly loves you, however, she will bite the dust.

## ✳ How To Make Him Fall in Love With You, Really

To Sag, life is a Noel Coward play, and if it's not, it should be. If he realizes he's surrendering to love, he'll put up a fight—a truly spectacular fight. Be aware that this will happen. He needs a companion who responds to love and adventure with the same breathless enthusiasm as he does, but he doesn't know this.

Sag doesn't really know what he wants, and he envisions marriage as something akin to the measles, bondage, indentured servitude, and the death of spontaneity.

So—you're having a ball together, he makes you laugh, you make him smile, you find each other endlessly fascinating to talk to, and you personally have *never* mentioned the word "marriage" or "wedding."

Gradually, it dawns on him how much more fabulous life can be when there's two of you. You, yourself, are too busy having fun to notice. Then one day, you go away! Where? He doesn't know. But you're gone for a week or two, and all of a sudden it hits him that you're seriously and deeply Not There. It then hits him that it's not measles after all! He's seriously and deeply in love with you! When you return, ignore the stunned look in his eyes.

## ✳ Make It Forever

Believe it or not, Sag makes a marvelous husband when he is deeply loved and deeply understood. He needs an extraordinary amount of mental free-

dom. Would he rather work at what he loves than
make a lot of money? Does he need to wander off
by himself occasionally, riding the rails of his
mind? The woman who understands this generous,
adventurous soul will be rewarded with an extraordinary love and eternal devotion. If you love him
with your whole heart, trust him completely. Like
Jupiter, his ruling planet, he will expand right before your very eyes into the wise, philosophical,
daring, exciting, devoted man he was born to be.

And lastly, if you love him, show him! At every
opportunity! Make your hugs, squeezes, pats, feels,
sneak attacks, and kisses an indispensable part of
his day.


## CRUCIAL MINUTIAE

### * What To Feed Sagittarius

Anything. Anything with flair, that is. A bowl of
chili over a campfire. Dark chocolate bars at the end
of a long hike. Grilled trout you've caught together.
Popcorn and toasted marshmallows over a roaring
fire.

Un-outdoorsy? Try biscuits and sherry in some
out-of-the-way pub you've lured him to. Subma-
rine sandwiches in the car on a rainy day when
you've kidnapped him for an adventure. Champagne cocktails as the two of you sit at a dark piano
bar, listening to Gershwin. A bag of peanuts at the
zoo. Sag needs food for the soul more than food for
the body—give him a bit of both and he'll trot happily by your side.

## ✳ How to Take Care Of Your Sag

Sag is a magnificently healthy beast who usually enjoys the challenge of the great outdoors. Rock-climbing, helicopter skiing, bodysurfing—whatever the sport, he'll try to coax you into it. Go along with him! He'll be thrilled at your sportsmanship and delighted to have your company. With his restless mind, however, he can overdo the party scene, so lure him to your lair for some indoor fun and sweet dreams together.

Any kind of massage is marvelous for Sag, since it will sooth his athletic muscles and calm his over-wrought mind. Introduce him to the inner adventure of meditation, which will help to chase away the blues. It's best to do this by giving him a few books on the subject, to get him intellectually interested in the bizarre idea of sitting still.

## ✳ For His Birthday

Tickets! To anywhere! Paris, Moscow, Japan. A witty play, an exciting lecture, a good movie. A surprise day (kidnap him from work) in the forest or park. An overnight inn at the beach. A horseback riding party. A row across the lake to some secluded gazebo. A bicycle built for two.

If you really can't go anywhere, think about giving him a puppy or, at the very least, a talking bird. Books are always welcome to this voraciously curious soul. And you might include a lottery ticket or even a night at the casino—Sagittarius is notoriously lucky. (And notoriously generous when he wins!)

# capricorn

## DECEMBER 22 - JANUARY 20

### BEST LOVE MATCHES

Capricorn & Taurus
Capricorn & Virgo
Capricorn & Scorpio
Capricorn & Pisces

He's standing quietly off to the side, appraising the success of the party. His party. He's the host, the mastermind, and the owner of all he surveys. He has exquisite taste, mega-ambition, and powerful desires. He's Capricorn, the Goat.

## FAMOUS CAPRICORNS

Elvis Presley, Martin Luther King, Jr., Edgar Allan Poe, Mel Gibson, Val Kilmer, Denzel Washington, Kevin Costner, Jim Carrey, Howard Stern, Nicholas Cage, Gerard Depardieu

## I AM

Seeking a companion, partner, mate. You will never find me at the center of the party—social pyrotechnics are so pointless. I am here, at the back of the room, where I can monitor the smooth, efficient progress of the meeting. And run smoothly it does, since I ran simulated test graphs on it early this morning.

Yes, it is a party, but I prefer to call it a meeting, since I intend to do some quiet business here. But that doesn't mean I haven't scanned every woman in the room in the hope of finding you. They say you don't exist, but I know you do. More than any other sign, I am looking for The One. You're the only woman who measures up to my standards. Value is everything to me. It took me ten years to acquire that painting over there. So what? Time is money, and money is time. In forty years, that painting will appreciate exponentially—but back to you.

Once I have chosen you, you may not know it for a while. I abhor unnecessary displays. When I open champagne, I take time to read the label, since the label is the best available. I appreciate the tiny chains of bubbles (tiny is better), and I relish them for the sheer sensual pleasure they can give me. Also for the sheer quality of the investment I made when I bought the whole case. I savor the first small sip, inhaling its perfume, perhaps letting a memory overtake me. You see, more than any other man, I have time. And I take my time. Everywhere. Think about that. So challenge me. Make it a little difficult. If you are not for everyone, then Bravo.

I am seeking a companion, someone I can talk to, preferably about politics, mutual savings accounts, sports, retirement funds, future plans, and insurance coverage. I may appear shy and reserved, but don't be fooled. There is a hidden room in my heart that only you will know how to uncover. I'll never tell you how, since I keep deep secrets, and if you've got the brains to figure it out, you've already lifted yourself above the herd. Good for you.

I take life seriously. I had a 401K picked out in kindergarten. I always wear galoshes. I consider what the neighbors think to be vital and important data. Some would call me cautious, I prefer the term selective. I have been accused of finding the meaning of life in a stable growth fund—this is ridiculous. The words "stable," "growth," and "fund" describe the kind of relationship I alone can completely appreciate.

I am a loner, a climber, and a planner. When I find you, you will be the jewel in my castle, and even if my castle is a one-room cottage, it will be built on bedrock, with a state-of-the-art security system and a million-dollar umbrella policy. The bedrock is important, since we are founding a dynasty.

Do not try to fool me, dear—I have exquisite radar. I will know if that sweater you're wearing is Merino wool, or a petroleum by-product. I am a simple man. I have one watch, but it is well-worn, classic, and looks like Great-Grandfather passed it down to me. Maybe it came from the flea market, but how charming that you should think otherwise. I may own only one car, but it won the car-of-the-year award in its class. I prefer one superb painting to rooms full of framed posters. Posters are for children, and I was never a child. No matter my current financial status—cheapness of soul or taste gives me heartburn. Do you find me diffident? So much the better. My aura eliminates the undesirables. I refuse to perform socially. I perform at work, where it counts . . . and elsewhere.

If I want you, you will have no choice in the matter. The word "no" does not exist to me. Sex is something that only improves with age, as you will find when we are in our seventies. I experience my love for you most deeply in the peak of physical passion, and I need you to want me as much as I do you. To be precise, I do not actually need you, but I want you more than you will ever know.

## YOU ARE

My companion, my hostess, my investment partner, my love. You are a diamond among rhinestones. You move like a ballet dancer, with grace and carriage. You wear pearls, even to the beach. You have flawless skin, since you started facials in nursery school. All the better to show off the magnificent jewel I will one day place around your neck—and you are that rare woman who will appreciate the gift and the investment value.

You are superb in the kitchen, and your kitchen looks like a Williams-Sonoma catalogue. You are a deeply sensitive sensualist. You were born to appreciate the best in life. You have a marvelous sense of humor, perhaps better than mine, but it is never vulgar. To protect your dear, shy heart, you have walls of reinforced steel. The hammer in the velvet glove, you are a totally feminine woman with a cool, practical brain. When I talk business to you, you talk back. Shrewdly.

You are untouchable. Every man in the room wants you, but they mistake your seriousness for ennui. I don't. You are reserved, a little aloof, thoughtful. The A student who wears black lace underwear. You're a first-class geisha in bed, but no man seems to interest you. I have to earn you, and I have never had to earn anyone. This role reversal stuns me. But you're the one I want.

You place the highest value on yourself. Your body is in impeccable shape. And even if it isn't, you act like it is. You have an exquisite manicure at all times. You have cashmere washcloths. You stoop to conquer.

## HOW TO DRIVE ME WILD

Don't make it too easy. Take your time. I like the value you place on yourself. But don't tease me if you don't mean it. I don't like wasting my time. Tell me honestly what you think and want; I'll know if you're lying. I like the way you look all virtuous and dutiful, with just the barest flicker of a hint of the wantonness beneath. I know it's there. I see it in that little half-smile. You've never been ignited by a man before, have you? I need to be the first to do that.

Did you know that I've been called a male chauvinist pig? How amusing. So I won't lower myself to appear lovable. So what. I just want to see how you'll move once you've decided you want me. I like you to figure out what I like. There are all kinds of little tricks I enjoy, and I like to be surprised. Within reason. I like that you've poured the Courvoisier into Waterford snifters. And I appreciate those candles. Real beeswax, aren't they? And this soft, handwoven blanket you've laid in front of a dying fire.

You're probably ready for me to make my move. Don't tell me what to do. I don't like that. I know what you want, and I will find out the rest. I'm a superb student. Let me undress you, slowly. When I have you naked beneath me—and I like you there, beneath me—let me see your pleasure. Tell me you like what I'm doing. You could run your breasts over my stomach, down into my thighs. Now run your nipple up through the hair of my groin and insert it into my navel. Continue to travel up my body. I'm sure you'll find other places. Surprise me with your sensuality.

Sometime you'll have to let me tie you up. Don't worry, we can trust each other. I just want to see you with an Hermés scarf tied over your eyes. Yes, like that. Gorgeous. Now turn around and kneel so that you're facing away from me, looking straight into a mirror. Maybe put your hands behind your back, if you won't let me tie them, too.

You are my beautiful, sensual, helpless slave, and I want you so badly I can barely control myself. But I do control myself. I will outlast you—tonight, tomorrow, and every other night. You will have your fill of me before I let myself go. I'm a climber, and I take my time. And I will take you up to the very peak of sensual pleasure. Now. And tomorrow. And for the rest of your life.

## CONFIDENTIALLY YOURS

### ✳ What He Won't Tell You

Yes, Capricorn is shy and reserved—as in Federal Reserve. The bottom line is the Holy Grail to this guy, and if you can adjust to this idea, your life will be increasingly secure. It may even be luxurious. Notice how he got off the subject (you) once he started figuring the yearly appreciation of his painting? Work is his first wife, and you are second wife, not mistress. (Mistress implies frivolity, and he's hardly into frivol.)

Another reason he works is for the pleasure of control. The Goat likes control. Over you, his family, and his job, and it doesn't matter if he's a house painter, an accountant, or a stunt pilot. He's not working, you say? Then either he's brooding about it, or duty is calling him elsewhere. If he has little power at work, then he'll get control in another realm. His home, for example, or his hobby. (Capricorns refer to hobbies as their "second career.") Don't judge him too harshly. His ruling planet, Saturn, is a stern taskmaster, and that's how Capricorns view life—as an unending series of dutiful tasks. It's all a poor Goat can do to keep up.

Capricorn is seriously into power, however, and power, when he can get it, makes up for a lot. He's the CEO, the owner of the castle; he's got the biggest pizza delivery route in town. "Acquisition" is his middle name. If he's a garage mechanic, he's making plans right now to buy the garage someday. Then he'll open a chain. He's a workaholic who has to have his jokes repeated to him, preferably diagrammed by an aide. He's a superb manager, no matter what his station in life.

The Goat's management skills extend to all forms of animate life, and he uses them freely to climb his way to the top. If you want an opinion on any subject, just ask Cap. Since he's humility-challenged, he probably won't wait for you to ask, and he knows his advice is second to none.

We hope you don't enjoy staying out til dawn, shedding various clothes and inhibitions in the process. Capricorns like their lives secure and serene— and early to bed, early to rise is serene. He prefers his socializing to have a purpose, and he needs a reason to party. Business would be best, making a connection would be OK, also learning something or even doing good unto others will suffice. Capricorns are into meaning. Fun has no meaning, which is the point of fun, which is why they don't get it.

## * The Bad Stuff

The Goat is never boring—to himself. But you may have to redefine the word to your friends. You will get on well with this guy if you remember that the meek (you) will inherit the earth—after his thousand-year reign is over. Forget all that nasty thinking you learned to do in graduate school—he will think for the two of you from now on. He may have champagne tastes on a beer budget, but if so he'll expect you to make the beer taste like Dom Perignon.

Cap says he's diffident—read "stone-faced." You've seen pictures of the carved gargoyles who peer down from the great cathedrals in Europe? They look as if they have indigestion, no one amuses them, and besides, it's raining? They were Capricorns. He abhors unnecessary displays—this includes spontaneous laughter, public display of affection, and witty jokes. He wants you to have a sense of humor, but within reason. And reason is way down the galaxy from whoopee.

And we hope you didn't miss that whopper about "I don't actually need you." Not! More than almost any other sign, Cap needs a mate. A mate gives him a reason for all that ceaseless toil. He functions better in a duo, and besides, he needs someone on twenty-four-hour call to cheer him up, since Capricorn's emotional weather is always Partly to Mostly Cloudy.

Fortunately, you don't like to be lavished with expensive gifts. "Money" and "lavish" never appear together in his sentence structure. "Money" and "careful" do. You've heard that children should be seen and not heard? So should women, according to Capricorn males. His (few) friends call him "Ol' Stonewall" behind his back. If you're a woman who delights in ministering to the one man whose personality could charitably be described as "impossible," then read on. This one's for you.

### ✳ How Capricorn Likes His Women

In his mind, he has the woman brought in for dessert, like Napoléon.

Tell him you are not dessert. Let him know as you search for dust on top of his stereo that you are the main course. In fact, he's your first course, and men never really get any farther than that with you. He likes intelligence, so you can speak your mind, but don't be vulgar and don't compete. Secretly, he's a Pygmalion freak—if you're looking to be molded, or if you have a bit of the waif about you (a well-mannered waif with clean, shiny hair who's just going through a phase), he'll be intrigued.

If you're an old-fashioned girl who's looking for Daddy, look no further. Particularly if Daddy was somewhat humorless, duty-bound, and gave orders well. But in return, you have to enjoy the stability, solidity, and security that he needs and will seek to provide. Some Cinderellas might find the castle routine pretty tedious on a daily basis. (Ask Princess Di.)

And don't worry about refusing Capricorn a few times. If he wants you, you will be hunted down and found, even if you abscond to Tibet. Besides, a well-placed "No" here and there lets him know your worth. Even if he seems interested in a weekend affair, he's secretly scanning you for marriage potential. So if you have a classic, thoughtful exterior, with a warm, practical core, give him a chance. He doesn't know it, but he's looking for someone who can warm his slightly chilly heart.

## ✳ What Cap Sees When He Looks At You

A worthy companion and partner, beautifully groomed. Someone whose portrait will suit the mantel over the fireplace. A superb hostess who will take equally good care of him on rare evenings when he's home early. Someone who doesn't laugh when he takes his *things* seriously. Remember, acquisition is next to godliness. Besides, he killed himself to acquire that computer-driven lawn mower that monitors grass growth all by itself, and it represents his status in the neighborhood. Cap needs a woman who places a very high value on herself. A woman with ambition, which he understands. And finally, a woman out of reach to anyone else but him, the Master of the Universe.

## ✳ What Turns Him On

Power. His own. So where do you fit in? Essentially, you don't have a price. You simply can't be bought. Refuse, and we mean really refuse, to be impressed by his implacable, towering, Saturnine self. (If he's short, it doesn't matter. He towers inside, or in his dreams he does.) If he intends to be rich, and he usually does, even if he was shucking clams when you met him, let it drop that you do, too. He's a mild-mannered accountant? Hah. He's planning a takeover—of his business, or you. Or both.

So, since he's all about power, be all about values. You'd like to go with him to that gorgeous restaurant—the one with Limoges fingerbowls—but you promised to take your nephew to the zoo six months ago, and you'd never go back on your word. But you won't be lonely, since you're rereading *Pride and Prejudice*. Jane Austen believed in marriages of quality and equality—oh, you'll explain the concept—and besides, her domestic scenes are so serene and somehow comforting.

P.S.—You've heard of the perfect lover—the one who turns into a pizza at 3:00 A.M.? A Capricorn male made that up. He likes sex—oh dear, yes—but at his convenience, on his schedule, and don't try to hurry him up because you have a breakfast meeting early in the morning. Let him know that you, too, have a schedule, and you, too, value your money, er, time. If he wants harmony in his life, he will have to learn to mesh schedules with you, his chosen. Notice we didn't use the word compromise. He can't spell it, so no use dragging it into the conversation.

## ✳ What Rules Capricorn

His mind, as long as he's using it to control. This gives you an advantage, since he's really kind of dumb in the heart department and needs a warm, tranquil presence to thaw that little igloo in his chest. What about his soul? Why bother with souls when you have a good mutual fund?

# THE CHASE

## ✳ His Secret Paradox

The Goat doesn't really want you to walk three paces behind him; it's just that he's so good at giving orders. And if you're not careful, you will. This man has been a consummate power broker since his first burp. But remember: absolute power corrupts absolutely. (Don't repeat this out loud; it would only confuse him.) The greatest antidote to power is love. The more you love your Goat, and the more you warm him up, the less power-brokering the two of you will need to do.

## ✳ How To Bewitch Capricorn

Nothing he does really impresses you, deep down, and you let it (yawn) show. You are, of course, extremely polite about his grasp of the current political scene, but you read it all last week in *The Wall Street Journal,* and, well, wasn't his analysis just a tad postmodern?

Hmmmm. He has his future mapped out? So do you, financially. Although in your heart you yearn for a simple life of quiet domestic bliss (so does he), your ambition just may prevent that from ever happening. You couldn't let a mere man stand in your way. You value yourself too highly. While values don't interest him personally—they are a means to an end—they impress him. So have a lot. When he takes you on a horribly expensive date, send him a thank you note, on good paper. It will drive him crazy, since he considers that he just bought a piece of you over the chateaubriand, and your proper little note signals that he didn't.

P.S.—Wear good, beautifully made clothes. But

be sure to let that handmade black lace teddy peek out of the gabardine jacket. What did he think you were? A nun? Let him know your sex drive matches his. Drop a reference to stamina, that great underrated virtue. If only, sigh, you could meet a man whose perseverance matched your own.

## ✳ Don't . . .

Gush. Dress punk. Spill JOLT cola on his well-polished shoes. Make bathroom jokes. Yawn a lot while he talks and tell him it's just a jaw relaxation exercise. Tease him in front of others. Tease him in front of his family. Tease him all alone on a desert island in the dark. Criticize. Ever. Buy pineapple Christmas tree lights that glow in the dark. Serve him Cheerios for dinner. Grow mushrooms in the corner of the closet. Tell him you enjoyed that teensy trinket from Tiffany's. Tell him "Enlightenment" means lightening up.

## ✳ Who He Likes To Bed

Capricorn can get rather confused about sex, lies, and everything in between. He is a desperately serious person, but learning that all that glitters is not gold may take a while. So if you just want him for the evening, glitter away. Be mysterious, classy, and out of reach. Throw hints of unspoken voluptuousness. Be the gorgeous glass mountain that 100 princes could not climb. (Remember he's a goat— he needs something to climb.) If you want to drive him insane, leave a dog-eared copy of the *Story of O* half-hidden beneath the bed.

## ✳ Who He Likes To Wed

Mom. But a subservient, sensuous Mom who will reflect his glory on her own. He has a shy and melancholy heart deep within that granite fortress. Capricorn is the sign of winter. It's not that his heart is frozen; it just didn't get past January. And January's sun isn't bright enough to coax the icicles from his breast.

If you can be elegantly practical, sensibly passionate, and nurture a secret feeling of romantic destiny (remember, you're The One), you're well on your way. And if you're warmhearted enough to dispel the Saturnine gloom, you'll go far. Display your common sense with pride. Have a sacred mission you need to fulfill—particularly one that involves family. Show that you adore propriety. Most particularly, take care of the child in him and he'll take care of all of you. Beautifully.

## ✳ What He's Secretly Afraid Of

Maybe underneath all that rabid overachieving, he's really rather ordinary. Perhaps that snickering in the next apartment was meant for him. The crabgrass is his fault, and all the neighbors know it. Was that a helpful hint or was he being criticized? Witty, charming extroverts have more fun. Life is short and then you die.

## ✳ When To Say Yes

Do not slip under Mr. Goat's tasteful, ironed sheets until he has to give up something to get you. Value, remember? You are beyond price. This will drive him mad, since "everyone has a price." Except you.

So resist. Don't tease, but do take your time. Check him out. Make him wait. Befriend him, seriously. He has the time, and he'll play along as long as there's a glimmer of real interest. Give him a test he has to pass—Saturn men love stern challenges, and achievement makes them feel fulfilled. You, personally, don't fall for just anyone. That would imply coming down to their level. You do, however, allow them to serve you, after checking out their intentions, credentials, and bank balance.

## THE COUP DE GRACE

### ✶ His Sexual Secrets And Desires

Is he visual, auditory, or kinesthetic? Capricorn's an Earth sign—so think kinesthetic. That means touch is of paramount importance. The Goat feels himself most connected when he's physically in touch. Shoulder massages, reflexology, the tango—they were all invented for Cap.

His center of gravity is probably low. And solid. He's extremely sensual, and sex is very, very important in his scheme of things. It's how he unwinds, lets go, and reaches the stars. (For unenlightened Capricorns, the act itself is more important than the person.)

Since quality means a lot, have silver candlesticks, excellent music, and Pratesi sheets (if they're not, they look like they are). If the floor is your choice, make sure it's well-cushioned. The Goat sees no reason sex should not be comfortable, especially since it will take a long time. Save the nipple rings for the Aquarius, but hide them well, since Capricorn does not like to feel outdone by any mortal rival. Since Caps have legendary stamina, however, don't be surprised if he whips out a device or two to prolong his pleasure. Don't be shocked. Be grateful.

This is a man who likes you to learn him, as he will learn you. He likes little surprises, so stick a pair of crotchless panties in his briefcase, where he can find them and think about you all day long. He's not averse to letting you do most of the work, initially; he stays in control because he comes when he damn well wants, not when you want. So seduce him. Slowly. Melt yourself into his arms and slowly move around the room to some good jazz. Now stop. Slowly stand before him and let your clothes drop to the floor. Begin to undress him, moving down his body as you go. When you are on your knees, gently reach up and pull him to you.

Once he's sunk down on your sumptuous cushions, massage his lower back, slowly, with your fingers, and then use your tongue. Turn him over. Try flicking your nipples all over his face and mouth. Let one nipple rest in his ear, and do it again in his mouth. But only briefly. Slide down and continue all over his chest; don't forget the navel. Now move your breasts over his groin. Lightly. Take your time. Break the rhythm so he can't predict what you'll do. When he's almost out of his mind, lower yourself onto his solid, well-built frame and use your whole body in one big massage motion. Up one side and down the other. Keep doing this until he's nearly crazy. You can come now, since he needs to prove he can satisfy you, as many times as you like. He won't climax until you're satisfied and he's decided he's ready. It's that stamina thing—he confuses it with ego. Lucky you.

## ✶ Shhh . . .

Leave a silk scarf hanging over the nearest chair, and tell him you're afraid of making too much noise. He gets unusually turned on by the sight of you, gorgeous, naked, and gagged. Simulate resistance. It'll turn him on even more. Anal sex is a known predilection of Capricorns. If you're up to it, suggest sometime that you're still a virgin, in places. And you wish someone would do something about it.

P.S.—Make sure that you really like sex if you want your Capricorn. Recall that this is the sign of the Goat. We say no more.

## AFTERGLOW: WHAT YOU NEED TO KNOW

### ✶ What Capricorn Likes Better Than Sex

Control. But you knew that. He's serious about sex, though, whether he's happily married or into multiple partners. But he won't give up control for sex. He may indulge in wild nights of hedonistic abandon—well, make that comfortable nights of well-regulated climax—but this is because you, the night, and the climax are part of his personal real estate, so to speak, and he's a hands-on manager. You see? Control again. If you need someone to emotionally dominate, look elsewhere.

### ✶ Will He Marry His Best Lover Or Best Friend?

His best friend, hands down. But Capricorn sees no reason the two can't be combined. He gets along best with an earthy, sensual companion who understands his pleasure. And one marvelous gift that Saturn gives to all his children is that they get younger as they age. Old Capricorns are positively flushed with youth.

### * What He Wants From You

Competence. Capricorn will expect you to function as well as he does in a variety of roles: wife, friend, advisor, listener, supporter, admirer, nurse, mother, hostess, geisha.

### * What He Needs From You

Warmth. The Goat's castle has a big, hand-carved hearth, but there's no cheerful fire crackling inside. He needs you to keep the *homme* fires burning.

### * What He Won't Give up For You

His dignity, his good name, his standing in the community, his bank account, his investment portfolio (if he's a starving artist, he's dreaming of an investment portfolio), his scheduled map of the future (he's planned his afterlife), his ambition, security system, insurance policies, career (dream on), ties to family, respect for authority, and church affiliations. And this is the short list.

### * What He Will Give up For You

What's all this talk of giving up, as if romance were some sort of power struggle? Capricorns do not have vulgar power struggles; they have power encounters. They win or they leave. No muss, no fuss. He would rather investigate how you can be incorporated—a favorite Capricorn word—into his carefully planned, neatly scheduled existence.

### ✷ How to Make Him Fall in Love With You, Really

Tell him to forget the expensive gifts—remember, *things* don't influence you, nor does dining in a small, quiet, superb restaurant. He is not going to impress you into loving him.

Wait and watch, like a dedicated hunter, for the part of him that's vulnerable. You won't see it for a long time, because he'd rather die than let it show. But that's the part you fall in love with. Maybe he's afraid he's unlovable, deep down. Or maybe he's afraid he's an ugly duckling who never turned into a swan. He's shrewd in business, but not in romance.

So when you fall in love with this hidden, unacceptable (to him) part of him, really truly love it, but don't exploit your victory. Wait until he surprises himself by falling truly, madly, deeply for you, too.

### ✷ Make It Forever

Even if he's a doctorate in biochemistry and you're a flower arrangement artist, make sure the Goat knows that your mind is the equal of his. Being intrigued with your intellect will stun him, since he's ostensibly looking for a trophy, not a companion. Hint that trophy-hunting is so '80s.

Then remark that there are seven kinds of recognized intelligence, and which one would he say he has? Oh. You have two.

If you think you want to marry this man, be sure that you have a real, ongoing life of your own, or you will be eaten alive. He can't help it—he needs someone to withstand the megaton force of his ambition and ego. Really, he needs to be saved from himself. Remember what Mr. (Warren) Beatty said about Mrs. Beatty: "I wanted someone to make me be good." Who would have guessed?

## CRUCIAL MINUTIAE

### ✷ What To Feed Capricorn

Capricorn loves a woman who knows how to entertain. Here's a man who will look forward to your homemade pasta, pâté au canard, and Grand Marnier soufflé. A born snob, Capricorn will bring an excellent bottle of wine to complement your efforts. And he'll enjoy it if your kitchen is well-stocked with quality essentials, such as Henckel knives that will last for years. Elegant table settings are a must, even on a picnic. Definitely bring out your best china; he'll notice and acknowledge it. Since there's a little boy in there who wants to be taken care of, find out what his favorite foods used to be—applesauce? Fig Newtons? And serve them to him on a rainy day.

### ✷ How To Take Care Of Your Goat

Bone up on the various antidotes to depression, since it's painfully easy for Capricorn to get lost in the dark miasma of his own thoughts. Massage him often, since he carries a great deal of nervous tension in his neck and back. He may scoff at meditation, but he'd like the calming, tranquil effects that regular meditation would have on his system.

If you invite him to a football game, have a pretty woolen blanket to wrap around your legs, and bring excellent beer. Don't forget soft napkins and warmed pretzels with mustard. Capricorn will feel beautifully taken care of by your attention to detail, which matches his own, and your pleasure in serving him will keep him happy for days.

## ✶ For His Birthday

When gift-giving, think elegantly useful. Capricorns go for class and quality, such as a cashmere scarf or the finest tool kit you can afford. We know Cap is a snob, so anything with social value that he can display will do nicely, like a monogrammed DayRunner of Italian calfskin. Capricorn's also sentimental and family-oriented, so a silver-framed portrait of his parents should go down well.

He's also an all-out entertainer, so try a pair of Baccarat snifters and a bottle of VSOP. And biographies of famous people who have made it to the top (especially against all odds) will definitely bring a smile to your particular Goat.

*handwritten notes:*
Lucien 2-17-48
Rushton
Dan 2-12-64
White
Guar 2-1-52
Keene

# aquarius

## JANUARY 21 - FEBRUARY 19

### BEST LOVE MATCHES

Aquarius & Libra
Aquarius & Sagittarius
Aquarius & Aquarius

He's gazing out the window at the star patterns while he talks a blue streak with two dozen friends. Is his mind a million miles away? No, it's right here, and it's focused on you. But he'll never let you know. He's Aquarius, the Water-Bearer.

## FAMOUS AQUARIANS

James Dean, Langston Hughes, Matt Dillon, Peter Gabriel, Axl Rose, Michael Jordan, Prince Andrew, Placido Domingo, Arsenio Hall, Garth Brooks, James Spader

# I AM

I've been called crazy—I take this as a compliment, naturally. Life is much more interesting viewed from the side or the back. Have you ever realized the retina records all images upside down? Exactly!

You don't wear leather? Good. You must be a vegetarian; you're not ravaging the animal nations for godless pleasures. I am looking for a lov—uh, I'm looking for a good friend. Sex is OK—I mean, sex can be fascinating, but if I can't make love to your mind, it's just another valve job; know what I mean?

You will have to stimulate me mentally. I want to watch you make the first move. And just because I allow you to do the preliminary work, don't ever try to dominate me, kiddo. So I come across as the Buddha of Broad Street—never mistake tolerance for submission. I don't obey. And never, ever try to manipulate me. Next to me, you don't know the meaning of the word.

I've been accused of being aloof, detached, and disinterested. Me! My concern for humanity is so overwhelming at times that it robs me of speech. Believe it or not. This just shows you the self-absorption of the average non-observer.

If I want you, badly, madly, you'll never know. I may have an unusual mind—I may have a bonsai farm in the cellar (you, too, can grow a rain forest)—but make no mistake! I'm 100 percent, unadulterated male. Displaying interest is beneath my hormones. Candidly, I find sending cards and flowers offensive. Why send needless pieces of paper, clogging up the mail, when I've made it plain how I feel?

What should you do if I want you? Don't...

move. . . . I've spent the evening surveying you, I've examined you from every angle, I've concluded things about your life you probably never knew . . . and I'll chase you in my mind until you walk over and catch me.

If I want you, it's because you exude a mystery that I can no longer bear. I must unravel you . . . I must find out exactly why you look and talk and smell and move the way you do. I need you to allow me to show you the tenderness that I hide from the rest of the universe.

I can't become who I fully am by myself, although I don't know this. I need you to bring out my tenderness, my passion (yes, it's there, ignore what you hear), and to surprise me with what love truly is. Love isn't really a game, but I don't know that. I've got spiritual love down; it's Eros I wonder about.

How will I know it's you? I'll wake up beside you and I'll just be there—no mental break dancing, no shiver of tristesse, no haunted, otherworldly feeling . . . I'll just be there. Beside you.

## YOU ARE

My friend. My first, last, and always friend. You are a magnificent conversationalist. When we talk, you can follow me through the labyrinth and come out the other side. You are easily bored. Furthermore, if I'm out on a mental limb somewhere, you don't feel stupidly ignored. And your extraordinary femininity drives me insane; the more feminine you are, the more male I become.

Housekeeping is less important to you than house-experiencing, and I don't have to explain that. You've never, ever wondered what the neighbors think—of you, I mean. You certainly wonder about them and their eccentric ways.

You perform superbly in crowds, which is just as well, since there's always a crowd. You don't demand public displays of affection; discretion is your byword. You are fiercely private. You don't need explaining. You know that Stephen Hawking's theory means that time can go backward if only you can find the right door. You have a laugh like wind chimes in late winter, and you can help me find what I'm looking for. I don't know what I'm looking for, but I think you can help me find it. You make me be real.

If I want you, you have to follow me through the looking glass, up the down staircase, and through the keyhole . . . I play the world backward sometimes, just for the fun of it. Do you get it? Will you come?

## HOW TO DRIVE ME WILD

Conquest is everything to me. Everything. So make it new every time. And don't make it easy. Most people's minds are an open book, don't you think? Close yours and throw away the key. See if you can drive me insane. And while you're at it, educate me. What did you say that woman taught you in France? Give me a little demonstration. See if you can shock me—it'll never happen, but I'll adore you for trying. Come at me; I'm right here, but come at me through your mind. The rest of the world doesn't understand that mind-blowing sex can happen between two fully clothed people standing together in a crowded room. Give that to me. Figure out how to do it and give it to me.

You're graceful, you have the fluid movements

of a dancer; this upsets my view of you as my favorite sidekick, but God, it's arousing. You can make the first move, but I'll make all the rest. Is that clear? I don't like to be dominated. Take my time? Foreplay is the reason we're here. I can get lost in your body, and I sometimes do. In the meantime. . . .

I'm going to give you your oral test. Take off your shirt so I can see that black bra with the nipples peeking through. No, don't take off the blindfold, dear. Mmmmm. Your nipples taste like strawberries. Let me have another taste. Nice. Sit in the lotus position, in front of the mirror, so I can see all of you. I understand you've hidden some grapes somewhere. Now I'm going to find them. But I can't use my hands. I'll start with your ear, and I'll work my way down. Are they in your mouth? No. Your navel? Mmmm. No . . . Ahh, here they are. But you'll have to be very, very still so I can get them out. Don't squirm. If you squirm I'll have to start all over. How many did you say there were? Three? Lie back. This will take a while.

## CONFIDENTIALLY YOURS

### ✳ What He Won't Tell You

Have you ever seen two squids mating? The delicacy, the ephemeral ballet, the never-to-be-repeated exquisiteness of it all—the sheer weirdness that all this heart-stopping beauty comes from a squid—that's Aquarius.

And what is all this "if I want you"? If?? He wants you so badly his teeth are chattering. How can you tell? He'll ask your roommate for advice on his goldfish. He'll invite you to a lecture on Hegelian theory and barely say three words all night. Why? Because beneath the sometimes weird exterior, he's seriously macho. He doesn't really want to be caught in your earthly, time-bound, possibly binding net, so he squirms and wriggles like a fish on a hook. Don't worry—if he's studiously ignoring you, he's hooked.

Curiosity may have killed the cat, but it can bring this man back from the dead. Give Aquarius a mystery, a riddle, an enigma to solve, and he's yours for life. Well no, not for life, but until he solves you. Then give him another one. Remember Scheherazade, and proceed accordingly.

Aquarius is his friends, or so it will seem. Hope you're convivial. One Aquarius we know introduced his beautiful blond bride to three striking females and told her that they were his closest friends and he hoped, not that she would like them, but that they would come to accept her.

Note, however, that Mr. Sociable probably has few deep companions of the heart. He moves too fast, skims too much, and disappears too often for true intimacy. He thinks of himself as extremely likeable, though, and he is . . . if you can play by his rules, after you've managed to figure them out in the first place.

No matter what his IQ, Aquarius has an unusual mind. His mind combines the precision of a computer with the thought explosions of an Expressionist painting. Why this is bad for you can be couched in seven little words: genius is the ability to justify anything. Hence the most common word used to describe this man is "crazy." Followed closely by "cold" (read computer-esque), "undependable" (his mind is solving algorhythms on Jupiter, and you expect him to remember dinner?),

and "aloof." He is not aloof—he is fiendishly re-
cording everything that goes on, and his emotions
are actually seething somewhere in there. But they
never, ever seethe in public.

## ✳ The Bad Stuff

If you're interested in this guy, you probably had
a crush on Mr. Spock, didn't you? "I love mankind;
it's people I can't stand" is the Aquarian motto.
Aquarius is against lots and lots of touching. Even
though he loves humanity, God forbid it should
breathe all over him.

Never apologize, never explain—this is his
credo. Explanation? Certainly! Which one? The so-
ciological, the philosophical, the parapsychological,
the intrinsic, the diagrammatic, or the extrapolated?
Apologize?! But his intentions were as pure as the
driven scientific inquiry! How dare you ask him
to—gasp!—*apologize?* (Give up now. Your blood
pressure will thank you.)

He's fascinated by you. And the kid who pumps
gas, and the mailman, and the bus driver he met
this morning. Aquarius's fascination is democratic,
it includes all sentient things. So hey, feel flattered
by his attentions; they're slightly more personal
than a double-blind study.

Other men may be plagued, haunted, or obsessed
with sex. How delightful that Aquarius should
be free of such problems. If you need emotional
intensity, if you crave long weekends of pure,
X-rated sex—flee!! Flee now and *don't look
baaaaaaaccckkkkk!!!!!*

The good part is that he is one man who will
finally see you as a whole person, not just a set of
hooters. The bad part is that after a while, you

would pay to be seen as a set of hooters. Just once or twice a year. Imagine slinking up to him wearing a see-through bodysuit and having him remark: Did you know that snakes have separate upper and lower jaws so they can gorge on prey twice their size, and that their stomach juices can take up to thirty days to digest a wild boar?

Always remember that you are falling in love with a scientist at heart. Scientists are not: sentimental, romantic, touchy-feely, amorous, passionate, or repetitive. Repeating especially bores scientists to death. Repeating how much he loves you (he's gone over that with you already), repeating just how fascinating you are (ditto), or repeating sexual positions. Honestly, sport, after you've plowed through the *Kama sutra*, what else is there?

## ✳ How Aquarius Likes His Women

You are his pal, but at the same time, you retain your own agenda. You are rational, temperate, and reasonable. You do not litter his life with sudden emotional showers, or ruin the clarity of his thought with daily soap operas.

Aquarius likes you, oh, not obviously domestic, but there's no harm in having good housekeeping skills on your résumé, right, bud? He would rather turn in his Libertarian party badge than admit it, but, see, if you keep the household machine quietly humming in the background, then he is freed for pure thought, his primary hobby. Not that he will not help you with chores. Take out the garbage? Certainly! He's invented a miniature forklift that wafts the garbage right through the kitchen window, slides down the side of the building, opens the garbage can lid, and packs it in. What did you think he was doing all those nights in the cellar?

You may feel neglected from time to time, you may feel like a laboratory specimen or a research assistant, but you will never, ever be bored.

### ✴ What Aquarius Sees When He Looks At You

His pal. His wonderful Girl Friday, who mysteriously keeps the refrigerator stocked and remembers the perfect scientific way to roll the toothpaste (his way). He's brilliant, bizarre, baffling, batty. You're gregarious, game, giving, gorgeous. You shine in a crowd. You're pragmatic, a realist who considers flowers on Valentine's Day a defect of the imagination. You much prefer a bag of jelly beans on a rainy Monday morning.

### ✴ What Turns Him On

Puzzles. Problems. Mysteries. To keep him intrigued, make sure there's a piece of you that he simply . . . can't have. It's not that you wouldn't give that part of yourself to him if you could, but you can't. So, nothing personal, OK pal? Besides, you've given him your heart, your mind, and most of your soul. Why does he need it ALL? He thinks he does, and will lie awake nights plotting to capture every single last cell of you. He would uncover your DNA code if he could. Mysteries drive him insane. Make sure yours is eternal.

### ✴ What Rules The Water-Bearer

The intellect. The elusive search for the timeless, humanitarian, ultimate answer. How can one person be both restless and stubborn? Well, he's stubborn about his restlessness. An air sign denotes airy, celestial, brilliant thoughts and conversation. After you've been theorized to death, however, you may feel that an air sign means just that—a lot of hot air.

# THE CHASE

### ✳ His Secret Paradox

Freedom is his greatest need and goal. But in his endless pursuit of it, he may miss the mysterious freedom to love and be loved—true intimacy. He wants freedom from you, yes, but he wants you to lead him past his ruthless, uncontrollable need for the next frontier, and down the quiet path into his own heart. He, himself, doesn't know the way.

### ✳ How To Bewitch Aquarius

He's probably fiercely thinking of you as his official First Buddy, so he doesn't have to be shocked by his own disgraceful fall into love, romance, and surrender. So talk, talk, talk to him. He needs to be mentally intrigued, and he wants to be filled with admiration for you.

Remember to be very, very feminine. This should tilt the balance from Admiration to Deep Swoon. Remember, when he's head over heels, you'll think he's allergic to you. He is all Yang, even though there's a CD-ROM in there directing traffic, and his hormones will cheerfully betray him in the presence of serious Yin. Challenge his mind, but put your faith in more southern places.

### ✳ Don't . . .

Gossip. Tattle. Snoop. Carry a fake Chanel bag and tell him no one can tell the difference. When he takes you to a restaurant, tell him you want to be seen at one of the important tables. Make fun of his mice experiments. Tell dirty jokes at breakfast. Insist that foreplay is for sissies. When he comes home and wants to talk, tell him you haven't been satisfied since dawn, and drag him to the bedroom. Dominate him. Hint that he's a bit of a wet fuse in the great combustion engine of life.

## ✶ Who He Likes To Bed

For Aquarius to give himself in sex with you, he must feel totally, utterly comfortable. He is capable of flings, however, when he's in his bored, fidgety, roving phase. So if it's just for fun, be witty, baffling, paradoxical, cryptic, and Eternally Female. Let it be known you can't be tied down, to anyone, ever. You're so restless. Doesn't anyone have adventures any more?

## ✶ Who He Likes To Wed

Himself, as a female. And why not? He wants someone he can do everything with—sports, travel, games, pure thought, adventure, rescue missions, discovery, invention, and creative fantasizing.

Thus he'd like someone innovative, brilliant, adventuresome, idealistic, people-loving, honest, and kind—i.e., himself at his best. Beware, however: domestic bliss is NOT one of this man's personal goals. To capture the trust of this wild animal, make the net so big he never knows he's caught. Never let him feel the strings. Aquarian males need to roam the range—and the range is several galaxies wide.

## * What He's Secretly Afraid Of

There won't be anything left to learn after he's forty. His true great love was the blonde who loaned him her spitballs in sixth grade, and he blew it. Boredom makes your skin turn green. Known life will end in 2010. He will never, ever find what haunts and calls to him, because it doesn't exist. Excessive thinking destroys brain cells. Self-love makes your fingers drop off. Einstein had no friends.

## * When To Say Yes

You would never guess it, but Mr. Democracy actually likes that old-fashioned verb "to conquer." Meaning, to conquer you. So do not make it all that easy for him. Make sure you're very, very good friends before it even occurs to you that he's male. Develop your companion skills, envelop him in marvelous conversation, and don't say yes until he's beside himself with desire.

# THE COUP DE GRACE

## * His Sexual Secrets and Desires

This guy can fantasize like no other male in the solar system. He's unshockable. Loves games. And he'll try anything.

Before you make love, have a long conversation with your Aquarius about erotic inclinations. Manage to tell him exactly what you like, and how you like it. Later, bid your Aquarius come into the bedroom. Have an ice bucket with chilled Mumm's. Have silk, linen, or flannel sheets on the bed—anything that will stimulate the skin receptors of this exquisitely high-strung animal. Ask him if he wants to play a game. Gently take off his clothes. Blindfold him, have him lie back on the bed, and firmly tie his wrists and ankles to the bedposts. (Use the frame underneath if you have no posts.)

Using a feather, tease his forehead, cheeks, lips, and especially his ears with it, and ease your way down. Tease him all the way down and around his penis—don't touch it—and go on down, down, down his thighs, his legs, and his calves.

While you're down there, tell him you're going to play Twenty Questions. Ease your way up into his thighs, take the feather under and around each ball, and down to his ass. Flick his penis with it, and then ask him if he's ready. When he nods, flick it again. Ask him if he's sure. Take your tongue and, starting at the base of his penis, move it slowly and deliberately up to the top. Ask him if he can remember that move. Does he need it again? Do it again. Ask him if he knows it by now.

Now ask him a question. Wrong answers get a feather. Right answers get a tongue. For your questions, ask him everything you just told him a few hours ago about what you really want in bed. For example, exactly where you do you like to be kissed? If he can't remember, whip him with the feather. If he gets it right, lick him in one long, slow stroke. Tell him you hope he gets most of them right. Otherwise you'll have to stop.

As you near the end of the game, gently push his legs wide open and massage the area between his ass and his balls with your fingers. Make sure his legs are wide open. Massage him with your lips and your tongue until he can't stand it any more. Feel when he is about to explode.

When he begins to arch his back in orgasm, take

a small handful of crushed ice and position it firmly against the area between his balls and his ass. Don't grind it in. You don't want to hurt him; you just want to send him to orgasmic nirvana.

When you're done, softly lick the sweat off his face. He shouldn't be able to move for a while.

## \* Shhh . . .

Leave a gloriously nude photograph of yourself in his sock drawer. Call him up late one night and tell him there's a surprise in his bureau. Hang up. Refuse to pick up when he calls back.

## AFTERGLOW: WHAT YOU NEED TO KNOW

### \* What Aquarius Likes Better Than Sex

Thinking. If you haven't grasped that by now, you probably don't belong together.

### \* Will He Marry His Best Lover Or Best Friend?

Where have you been? You can't get to first base with this man, let alone back to the dugout, unless you're friends with him, his plants, his trained spider, his coworkers, siblings, acquaintances, dentist, medical technician, insurance agent, mechanic, and pharmacist. Just as well, since they're all coming over on Sunday for a barbecue. How's your grill technique?

### \* What He Wants From You

True-blue friendship, followed closely by mental stimulation. Through rain and sleet, through thick and thin, you're his unswervingly loyal, affectionate, intelligent companion. Kind of like Man's Best Friend, only you have other possibilities Rover couldn't begin to offer.

## * What He Needs From You

Privacy. Freedom. He needs to spin along his own planetary path, with you humming comfortably just a few light years away. If you grant him privacy, he will learn in time to open that data bank in his chest and find a true, loyal heart within. Show him that "intimacy" and "asphyxiation" do not mean the same thing.

## * What He Won't Give up For You

His friends. (Warning: if you're a real introvert, escape now or rot in social-talk hell for the rest of your life.) His privacy. The fact that he was right about that recycling argument you had five and a half years ago. The fact that you, the President, the Western Hemisphere, and China need to change, but he does not.

## * What He Will Give up For You

If it's right, he'll give up his lonely dream/memory of Her, She Who Lives Not On This Plane. This is a holograph of—you guessed it, his first love, as well as an undefined vision of Her which he has carried around with him since he was born. And seriously thinks he will meet someday. Teach him that it's Here-Now-You, not Where-Why-Who, and you will have won a glorious victory. For both of you.

### ✳ How to Make Him Fall in Love With You, Really

Be true. Be kind. And stay by his side. Aquarius lives in his mind, where he entertains himself endlessly, but he can get so abstract that he misses what's really real. This man needs to find eternity in a grain of sand, and he needs you to show it to him. When that happens, he can be incredibly tender, gentle, and courageous.

To get him to take you along on his crusades, be the friend he's always dreamed of, and is not, in fact, himself. Have just as much at stake in his causes as he does, since you can't fake this stuff for a lifetime, but retain your dazzlingly individual self. After all, that's who he fell in love with in the first place.

### ✳ Make It Forever

Remain true to yourself, *first*, and then to him. Do not become yet another crossword puzzle he happens to solve on pit stops between the asteroids. Make sure he knows that, although he can lead, "follow" is not exactly what you do. Sheep follow; companions march along side by side. Do not kneel to this guy. Let him unbar the door to his secret place and come out to meet you, unarmed with intellect, theories, or wit, and let him know that that is where you will begin your life together.

## CRUCIAL MINUTIAE

### ✳ What To Feed Aquarius

A large bowl of popcorn for breakfast—tell him the fiber's good for him. For lunch, a loaf of bread, a bag of cashews, and thou. Head for the hills. The cloud patterns will be your repast. And he has a hidden taste for the finer things. So smoked salmon with a bottle of Corton-Charlemagne should go down well. And have chamomile tea and soothing comfort foods on hand for when his nerves go on red alert. He can actually forget he has a body. Try to get him off caffeine (this is one sign that doesn't need it) and into light teas and vegetable juices. If he's stubborn, get him interested in the cellular regenerative properties of juicing and you should have no problem.

## ∗ How To Take Care Of Your Water-Bearer

This man's nervous system would wipe the smile off Mona Lisa. Beneath that lucid, rational exterior is a seething mass of crossed and desperate neurons, tripping all over themselves in an attempt to keep firing.

So give him a soothing massage once a week, and start meditating. (The best way to get Aquarius to do anything is to start doing it yourself.) He tends to use his body as a late-model vehicle for transporting his thoughts. So set up quiet little rituals, such as "breakfast," "lunch," and even the occasional "nap," and make sure he observes them. What you're trying to prevent here is neurological burnout before the age of forty. Invest in a book of Chinese medicine and explain to him the ageless benefits of Tai Chi. After all, think of the adventures you could have in your nineties!

## ∗ For His Birthday

Consider one of those star machines that light up your living room ceiling with the correct astronomical patterns. He'll love studying the stars in their various rotations and the whole idea of it will appeal to his sense of space, er, romance. Or sign him up for the first commercial flight to the moon.

Subscriptions to ecological and alternative magazines will also stimulate his interest. Send him a love note on the Internet. A good introductory book in a field he doesn't know such as archeology, ancient spiritual traditions, or folklore will delight him, since you're acknowledging his intelligence and curiosity.

Want to send him out of his mind? Investigate those travel/study trips (they're cheaper) to impossible places. You know, where he has to paddle up the Amazon in a dugout he made himself, and then meditate by the light of crocodile teeth for three days with an ancient forest shaman. After this, his mind is so expanded that he lies in a hammock in the treetops, while his brain goes on a cosmic trip he has never before experienced. At journey's end he will be sick as a dog as he paddles downriver, home, toward you, but he will be in speechless awe of your understanding of his true nature. And he'll have already signed up for next year.

○((●))

# pisces

_Andy_
_2-27-53_

## FEBRUARY 20 - MARCH 20

### BEST LOVE MATCHES

Pisces & Taurus
Pisces & Cancer
Pisces & Scorpio
Pisces & Capricorn

He's sitting quietly on the sofa, while three women sit at his feet. He's soft-spoken, romantic, and he's got fabulous eyes. He's Pisces, the Fish.

## FAMOUS PISCEANS

Bruce Willis, Kurt Russell, George Harrison, Jon Bon Jovi, Sidney Poitier, Kelsey Grammer, Lou Reed, Tom Arnold

## I AM

Looking for someone to change my life. If she wanted me to move to another city, change professions, change my name—well, my God! the adven-

ture! Don't you think? You don't? Oh. What do you
think? Why don't we retire to that sofa behind the
plants and you can tell me all about it. I adore listening. I could listen to you all night.

You're very beautiful; you look like someone
who enjoys being ... in control. You're probably
taken, though, aren't you? If you want, come with
me. Now. Don't hesitate. I don't like hesitation; I
don't see the point in waiting for pleasure. I have
a bottle of Château d'Yquem in the car. I'll wait for
you on the terrace.

Some have called me lazy. Pfft! I am an artist of
time. I can make a minute stretch into eternity. I
can wrap a weekend around you until you think
you've been away for a year. I can squeeze days
into hours in one long, immortal night. Let me
show you.

If we run away tonight, you'll get to see my vintage Jaguar sedan—it's a little weatherworn but it
feels so good inside. I rescued it from a junkyard
and I've been unable to part with it ever since. I
take care of things. Like Saint-Exupéry's Little
Prince, I realize that it is the time you spend wa-
tering your rose, and protecting her from the
worms, that binds your love for her. I know this
secret of the heart, and, oh, so many others. Let's
run away tonight. You don't have to be anywhere
tomorrow, do you? Are you with anyone? Does
that matter?

I want you because you seem the very echo of
someone I knew once upon a time; I don't know
which life. And because you look like you know
the way home. I don't, and without you I may
spend my life aimlessly wandering. I'm looking for
someone to do it all for—love, live, produce, create,

nest. I can't seem to do it for myself, but it would be my greatest joy to give it all to you.

## YOU ARE

Delicate in all the right ways. Your eyes are Pre-Raphaelite; your hair feels like the wind on a summer beach. Your skin is so impressionable you can feel starlight on your fingers. You wear a scent that drives me crazy, but I can't place it. You bring out my masculine side, and that is—so necessary! It's not that I'm not masculine; it's just so tiresome to flaunt one's testosterone twenty-four hours a day. I leave such exertions to those a little further down the food chain.

If I put you on a pedestal, it's because you deserve to be there. If I worship you, it is because it is in my nature to worship.

You have a dominant streak? So much the better. Although you are romantic, mystical, ethereal, you have a sturdy practicality about you that I crave, having none of it myself. You understand the appalling mysteries of an IRA, a six-month CD, and a portfolio spread. You have actually balanced a checkbook. You will never teach me this, God forbid, but you will balance ours, beautifully. Yet you do not consider finance to be an especially masculine vocation, and this is only one of your haunting charms. You have thoughtfully planned our future, a process that bores and frightens me, and I adore you for it.

You are a marvelous homemaker, and you have old-fashioned values. When I step into your kitchen I always feel welcomed and, better yet, fussed over. Being with you makes me feel snug and secure, like being inside by the fire on a cold, rainy night. It rains a lot where I live, or if it doesn't, it feels that way. You have an optimism about you that carries me along when I'm under a cloud, and I'm frequently under a cloud.

Sometimes, my dear, you are in danger of becoming my drug, but what a lovely habit.

## HOW TO DRIVE ME WILD

If I want you, I have chosen you for your exceptional sensuality, and for the sign in your eyes that you know. I don't need to tell you what you know, do I? What matters is that we both recognize it in each other. But when I ask you to come with me, don't turn coy. I don't like those kinds of games.

I'd like you to close your eyes and let me look at you . . . all night long. The sound of the fountain outside our window (there must be a fountain) will mingle with your dreams.

The next night—but why wait? Don't go to work! Stay here and we'll have oranges from Seville and handmade chocolates and a glass of Roderer for breakfast. I'd like you to feed me . . . why not take that silken scarf and wind it around my hands, and let me work for it. Would that please you? Would you like to see me squirming, naked and tied, picking up the chocolate with my mouth? Then I can feed it to you. And after you've had enough, you can tell me when I'm allowed to eat. This is one of the games you will bring to me. And I'll follow any desire you have. Any one at all.

Since we'll have breakfast around four o'clock in the afternoon, it will last until dark . . . and when it gets dark, light a candle and read to me. I want to feel your voice on my skin.

There's a marble bath next door, and I want you

to take me there. I want to lie back in scented water
while you run a soft brush over my skin. Don't take
your eyes off me while you do this. Tell me what
you think of my body. Tell me that I please you.
Tell me that you want me. Take me to the bedroom
and tie my hands again. I'll do the same to you
after midnight, if you want me to. But I want you
to see what I look like as a slave. There's a threshold of pain—that moment that threatens to explode
into agony before it turns into infinite, exquisite
pleasure. And you intend to take me there. Now
that you have me helpless before you, I want to
watch you smooth almond oil over your skin and
mine. I like the way we glisten in the moonlight.
When you lick the oil off my penis, don't use your
teeth. No, I said don't. Please. Please don't. Please
don't. Please. Please.

## CONFIDENTIALLY YOURS

### ✴ What He Won't Tell You

The Fish doesn't think ambition is necessary or
even good for one's health. After all, who won that
stupid race—the hare or the tortoise? And what on
earth were they racing for to begin with?

Although Pisces does well in careers that allow
him to be free, unfettered, and his own boss, the
Fish is mostly "not terribly"—not terribly ambitious, not terribly demanding, not terribly aggressive, dominating, steady, secure, energetic, or firm.
But the secret of life is enjoying the trip, isn't it?
Isn't the eternal *now* all we really have? Of course
it is. Pisces knows this better than anyone, so let
him take you along for the ride.

He is modest, self-effacing, and loves to serve. He

makes an excellent courtier or troubadour ... Like
the ones who hung around outside those twelfth-
century castles and sang of their undying love for
a mysterious, unattainable Lady. Not an especially
productive life, but God, it was romantic. They
were Pisces.

You note how he drags in Saint-Exupéry to justify his codependent relationship to his car. The
Fish is mentally unbalanced when it comes to lost
causes. One Pisces we know bought a used boat,
which he purchased on impulse, of course, because
he liked the name ("Foggy Wanderer"). The boat
sank whenever it got wet, but hey, what price poetry? Three years and $6,000 later, the boat still
hasn't spent the night in actual water, but he's con-
sidering a new forward valve before he replaces the
engine.

Give up? What?! After this kind of sweat equity?
How unfeeling can you be? Obviously, he can't explain it to you. That's because he can't explain it to
himself, so he rigorously bypasses such nasty logic.

Another Fish we know had a fourteen-year-old
car (a BMW, of course) that broke down once a
month. For eight years. Every tune-up cost $300. He
put his mechanic's children through college. When
challenged about this hopeless quest, he would
sigh, "Well, I've gone this far, you know...."
$27,000 (yes) later, it blew up in the middle of a
four-lane freeway, and he was forced to buy a new
one. So did he shop around, get the best price?
Nooo. Pisces are a salesmen's wet dream. The Fish
walked pliantly into the showroom, picked out a
color he liked, and paid full price, in cash, without
a peep. That would have meant haggling, and haggling gives Pisces indigestion. It wiped out his sav-

ings account, but why do you harp on finance? How crude! Money will waft in from somewhere. It always does.

Pisces would adopt a cockroach, if it seemed abandoned and starved. If you find a stray puppy, call this man and tell him there's a helpless creature that's only hours from annihilation, and could he baby-sit for a day or two? It's sneaky, but it works. Visit him in a week and the abandoned one will have a color-coordinated doghouse and a personal trainer.

The Fish is desperately frisky with the truth. There is "the" truth, your truth, his truth, and then there is the fib. The demi-fib. The non-fib. The well-intentioned fib. The fib he would have told you if you hadn't looked so sad. The fib he did tell you. The fib he gallantly withheld from you, thereby letting you assume something else entirely. Truth is so fractious. Too tedious, really, for the glorious Piscean imagination. Tsk. Why not tell it the way it should be, instead of the way it actually is? This is the special form of Piscean magic. To the untrained mind, it is also the special Piscean form of perjury.

Wedlock? One Pisces we know lived with a beautiful woman for three years. When she finally broached the subject, he was shocked. Marriage? To each other? Why no, it hadn't crossed his mind. Had it crossed hers? Did she have any reason for this sudden drastic inquiry? She did, and she went elsewhere for an answer.

Another Pisces we know is in his forties—a handsome, sentimental bachelor. He'd like to be married with children, sure, but *Mon Dieu*, the mess. What if he needed to read while they were teething?

## ✶ The Bad Stuff

You think you know all about passive aggression
from your ex-mother-in-law, right? Wrong. You
haven't been treated to the master of the art. Before
you argue with the Fish, practice biting savagely
into thin air. Your teeth will hurt, but you'll be
mentally equipped for Piscean warfare.

When roused, Mr. Fish lets loose a stream of po-
etic, right-brained invective, much like a disturbed
squid, and then scoots away beneath the murk he's
just created. This can be excessively annoying. Most
of us would rather be fought with than watch
someone leak away during an argument. Imagine
trying to punch a jellyfish. No contest, right? Just
remember as he oozes into the muck—he won.

One thing to quash immediately is his talent for
prevarication. When you want to know where he
was last night, You Want To Know Where He Was.
Not what the Big Dipper looked like, how the starlight reminded him of you, and by the way how is
that sore throat? Here, he's brought you organic
honey for your tea, shall he make you some? Not
before he drops the charisma right then and there
and tells you Where He Was. Then he can make
you a whole pot of tea and feed it to you spoon by
spoon.

Can he feel sorry for himself? Is rain wet? In fact,
the phrase "wet blanket" was invented by the
many friends of Pisces to affectionately describe his
approach to life. Did he make $100K this year?
Won't last. New house? Took all his savings. Great
relationship? She hasn't met the real him. Pessi-
mism is a religious experience to the Fish, and he
will fight tooth and nail to keep that sopping wet
blanket wrapped tightly around his rainy, mossy
heart.

Furthermore, the word "money" causes his delicate membranes to heave in protest. Money, like fine wine and tickets to the opera, should be handed to you when you're in the mood, preferably by a silent robot. But *earn* it? You mean he has to *think* about this? For how long?? More than a day??

## * How Pisces Likes His Women

On a magic carpet. Just like he likes his money, invitations, and bottles of Château Lafite. Few women arrive this way, however, so since he may have to extend himself for you, be sure you're the one he's been dreaming about. Thus, you are a woman who can bring out the male in any man with the exquisite finesse of your approach. Yet you have a delightfully dominant side that intrigues and draws the Fish like a glowworm on a hook.

You are an old-fashioned romantic. For you, there cannot be enough sterling roses on Valentine's Day—even if you have to buy them yourself because he's temporarily short. You have the practicality of a French housewife; you can prepare breakfast, refinance the house, and amortize your insurance payments, and yet you still consider it his job to pop the champagne cork at dinner.

You understand the spiritual meaning of money. When Paris beckons, the leaky plumbing can wait. You never, ever, ever nag. You, the Statue of Liberty, hold aloft the flame of eternal faith in your beloved, right up there where he can see it every time he feels blue, which is three or four times a day.

## * What The Fish Sees When He Looks at You

Sleeping Beauty. She who lives in a dream and wakes only to continue it, with her Prince. You are the magical one who can make home and hearth both stimulating and tranquil, sensual and snug, casual and safe.

While you are a witty conversationalist—Pisces, like Aquarius, needs up-to-the-minute stimulation—you are not an Italian opera. Not for you the daily drama, the emotional hysterics of an Aries or Leo. Your soul, though deep, projects the unruffled calm of a Swiss bank. To the delighted Fish, you are the North Star, which beckons him to foreign planets and guides him home again.

Pssst! Just because he is not brimming with ego, do not assume he is not strong. Although sometimes his strength seems weird for a male, remember that water is stronger than fire. Never, ever try to wear him out—you will end up a mere shadow of your former self.

## ✷ What Turns Him On

Sensuality. That gleam in the eye that tells him you've been there, and you'll take him with you. And just occasionally, he might have to obey, boy, got that? However, playing Mistress Lascivia and her Splendid Slave once in a while does not mean you are the belligerent type. (Besides, he's just as happy to chain you up, if that's what you desire.) If you are a terribly aggressive woman, stay away. You'll give him sexual heartburn.

Go slowly. Make it delicate, intelligent, and light. Let there be moonlight. Let there be pillow talk, and interesting, exploratory kisses. Let him see the halo of the eternal feminine hovering around your eyes, but never talk about it and never explain. It will make him feel as if he's finally found the girl who's been haunting his dreams.

## * What Rules The Fish

New experiences. In fact, he'd like at least a dozen a day. Since the fish must remain free to do all that experiencing, this can lead to an especially streamlined life. Buy a suit and tie? Why, he's thirty-five, never bought one yet! Why break with tradition? Besides, it might lead to something . . . domestic. There's safety in blue jeans and an up-to-date passport.

# THE CHASE

## * His Secret Paradox

He seeks the freedom of the open sea, but he yearns for a snug harbor. He's really looking for the woman in the song "You'd Be So Nice to Come Home To." Be his lighthouse. Be the sign that there is safety and happiness despite the storm, and his ship will rest safely in your harbor for many moons to come.

## * How To Bewitch Pisces

Listen to him. Take him seriously. No one else does. He can be extremely verbal, witty, and charming. But he's shy, and, deep down, not extremely sure of himself. Your steady, charmed gaze will prove to him that he is as fascinating as he secretly hopes. In fairy-tale terms, Pisces is the frog with the feet of gold. Your attention, your belief in him, and your calm, unwavering affection can transmogrify him from a horny toad to a dazzling Prince, ready to take possession of his kingdom with you at his side.

Need to practice unconditional love? Look no

further. Magical things happen when you love your Pisces without the "ifs." If he had a steady job. If he made $60K a year. If he'd grow up and drive a real car. If he'd stop that annoying habit of keeping unimportant secrets—you thought anal retentive went out with the '80s. Oops! You see how tempting it is. But keep your need to improve, shape, and guide his future locked in the bottom drawer of your mind. He needs the right environment before he can flourish, and if you can provide it, he will reward you with a tender devotion that you thought existed only in fairy tales.

## ✳ Don't . . .

Demand to see his portfolio before you sleep with him. Criticize. Repeat helpful hints more than once. Repeat respectful requests more than once. Inform him that if he really loved you, he'd tell you all those stupid secrets he keeps to himself. Make fun of his pet mouse. Tell him exercise is a great antidepressant. Leave *The Peter Pan Syndrome* on his coffee table.

## ✳ Who He Likes To Bed

How much time have we got? If you're feminine, witty, sensual to the max, and looking for an affair to remember, this is it. A word of caution: beware—he's oh-so-easy to fall in love with!

If you want to get away from it all, go Fish. If you want to forget about food, clothing, the cat's dinner, incoming faxes, your friends, your mother, your life . . . if you want it all now! Now! in an erotic rapture where there are no ties, no boundaries, no limits . . . if you want to charge your entire $6,000 weekend on your poor little wheezing credit card, he'll help you sign on the dotted line. Don't worry about paying it off. He never does. Have another bottle of Dom. There are dark corners of desire in your soul that you never even suspected. He knows. He's seen. And he'll take you there, again and again and again. Are there secrets of wisdom in excess? Pisces thinks so. Roll over and he'll reveal them to you.

## ∗ Who He Likes To Wed

He doesn't like the idea. Well, maybe, if you're a sensuous, discreetly assertive woman with a taste for adventure who can infuse him with Purpose. But really, why bother with marriage? Why not just stay as we are, undefined, unconfined, unentwined? If he absolutely *has* to, he'll look for someone who is ultra-sensitive, delicate, dreamy, wise, and financially stable. In other words, his ideal self.

## ∗ What He's Secretly Afraid Of

Marriage? He's only forty-three! Too young to die!! Ambitious, driven men have better sex. He really is a zero in the great spreadsheet of life. His living room and bathroom are being monitored, and his personal life will be featured tomorrow morning on *Oprah*. You create your own reality, so he must have chosen this mess. There are no second acts. There's a more interesting life around the corner. He peaked at three.

## ∗ When To Say Yes

Sooner rather than later. For all his daydreamy ways, the Fish doesn't like to wait for his pleasures.

In fact, he gets downright snappish. It's hard to call because he can be so casual and intuitive about you. (Warning: even if he looks good enough to eat, think twice if you prefer triple chocolate crunch. This man is definitely creme caramel.)

## THE COUP DE GRACE

**✳ His Sexual Secrets And Desires**

Make it near water. The sea, a lake, a pool, or even a bathtub. But make sure there is water near him, so he can hear it, smell it, and feel it on his skin.

He's extraordinarily sensual and he loves to play. So let there be candlelight and music. While you are both lying on your pine-scented bed, sipping vintage Krug, feed him a bowl of strawberries. But don't use your hands. Tell him it's a game, and whoever drops the most strawberries has to pay the penalty. When he's had enough champagne, tell him he lost. For the rest of the evening, if he wants to come, he has to ask your permission. And if he doesn't please you, you won't allow him to come.

Slowly smooth a light film of scented massage oil over his chest and down his thighs. Using your fingers, lightly twist his nipples back and forth. Tell him his hands are too free. You don't like that. Tell him to raise his hands above his head, and then cuff them together.

Now slowly strip in front of him. Remove your blouse; you're wearing a bra with the nipples peeking through. Take off your skirt—but linger—and show him you're wearing crotchless panties. Tell him he has to eat you, but if he doesn't do it right, you may have to blindfold him. So he'd better be good.

Now straddle him and wiggle your crotch up his chest until you move into position. When you climax, tell him he didn't quite lick you to your satisfaction, so you'll have to blindfold him. Gently place a black silk mask over his eyes. Now sit on his face again, and tell him not to be bashful this time. Tell him exactly how you like it.

Did you have fun? Tell him he's been good. He doesn't know how good. So you're going to do something to enhance his pleasure. Reach down and place a tiny clamp on each nipple—the kind that screw in. Turn the screws just enough to tweak him. Remember, he can't come without your permission.

Now gently lower yourself onto him; take your time. Begin to rock back and forth. When he asks you to please let him come, tell him you can't hear him. Reach around and graze his balls with your nails, lightly. Make him ask you again. Louder. And again. Louder. Tell him you want him to beg. When he's all gorgeous and desperate and begging and you decide it's time, lean down and kiss him on the mouth, and put him out of his misery.

## ✳ Shhh . . .

Next time you're undulating on top of him and he's in the close-to-oblivion stage, use your nails across his neck and chest. Just do it enough so that he feels it. Then briefly draw your hands across your face in the dim candlelight, and let him see some discreet blood. (It will be fake, of course, but the feel of your nails on his chest and the power of autosuggestion will make him think he has crossed the pain/pleasure threshold and he will pass out in ecstasy.) This little illusion will also work quite well for Scorpio.

## AFTERGLOW: WHAT YOU NEED TO KNOW

### ✳ What Pisces Likes Better Than Sex

Meandering. Pisces's true great love is Life herself, in all her thousand, beckoning disguises. He was going to be a seismologist, but he had to go to Brazil because Sarita was afraid to fly alone. It's been three years, but hey, he speaks fluent Portuguese. He'll come back someday, of course, maybe, but right now he's helping Martina out of her marriage, but then her sister Alicia got jealous and almost killed herself, and he couldn't let that happen, so, well, it's kind of complicated. So he can't leave just yet. In the meantime, he's selling his paintings on the beach, and he's been accepted at Clown School in Rochester, New York. Are you beginning to get it? Life is his secret, intoxicating mistress. He's so enthralled by the trip that getting anywhere is purely serendipitous.

### ✳ Will He Marry His Best Lover Or Best Friend?

A perfect blend of the two, with Lover perhaps pulling a slight lead. Unlike Aquarius, Pisces does not seek to marry a pal. The Fish needs romance, in and out of marriage—so take the hint and keep it in. On the other hand, she has to be a true friend, since the ideal wife for Pisces provides him with a sense of permanence and security, which we seriously doubt he finds in his love affairs.

## ∗ What He Wants From You

More than any other sign, Pisces needs to be understood. Turn up your intuition as high as it will go, and tune in to this man's unique take on all forms of life. He would not describe himself as passive; to him it's simple conservation of energy. And his easygoing, *comme-ci comme-ça* perspective? Sound economics—of emotion, that is. Why expend all that effort? Let's sit here in the back row and watch everyone else go crazy.

## ∗ What He Needs From You

Direction. The Fish needs a sense of security and permanence from you, and the feeling that you know where you're going. But his attitude will put you in a double bind. He'll tell you to write that novel, but then he'll tell you how few get published each year, the odds are staggering, too bad you don't have an agent, it would be so much easier, but agents are such harsh creatures, who would want to associate with them, he really admires how you're going to find the time to do all this when you already have a job and your fatigue level is rising. . . . No, go ahead! You're so talented!

P.S.—He can be casual, oh so casual. Put a stop to this nonsense and let him know that now-you-see-me, now-you-don't, does not a great love make.

## ∗ What He Won't Give up For You

His privacy. Ever. His dreams. The secret knowledge that he could escape from it all, if he really wanted to. (And he can, so make sure he doesn't really want to.) His cozy sense of doom. His en-

dearing, hopeless generosity. His certain knowledge that things are bad and getting worse as we
speak.

## ✶ What He Will Give up For You

His restless search for the ultimate high. His need
to peek around just one more corner. (Tell him you
like corners too, and go with him.) His belief that
"wedlock" means just that—locked in wed. Let
him know you trust him completely—you know he
will return after all his mental and physical wan-
derings, and he will have no need to wander very
far at all.

## ✶ How to Make Him Fall in Love With You, Really

Pisces can make you feel the way you felt at six-
teen, with your first love, when all the world was
new. You are that rare woman who respects a man
for his soul, not his bank account. You are ever
ready to run away with him, even in your eighties.
You adore the elegance of his approach, and you
are sure of yourself. You allow him all the explor-
ing he needs—which he finds, after all, is not very
much. Your Fish is overjoyed to find you, for you
let him know that he is loved for who he is, which
transforms him into who he wants to be.

## ✶ Make It Forever

Make it serene. Make it secure. Make it compas-
sionate. Teach him that intimacy is not torrents of
emotion, psychic vibes, or spiritual hankerings.
True intimacy is grounded, simply, in everyday life
with you. You understand him and you love him;
you see everything about him and you still think

he's the most marvelous man on earth. Never violate his privacy. Trust him completely, and he will live up to it a thousandfold.

## CRUCIAL MINUTIAE

### ✱ What To Feed Pisces

Feed his soul at the same time you're feeding his body. For breakfast sometime, cook up some kippers and rashers of bacon, with a pot of strong tea. Play Renaissance music and tell him you're dying to go to Devonshire this summer. His imagination will wake up with a bang, and so will his metabolism.

This kind of breakfast is useful for Pisces every once in a while—he needs beefing up, especially after a night of heavenly excess with you. Since the Fish has a serious yen for the finer things, spoil him by spooning Beluga into his oh-so-kissable mouth on crisp little toast points. Wash it down with vintage Krug. Kiss him only if he smiles.

### ✱ How to Take Care Of Your Fish

Massage is a must. It's sensual, intimate, and best of all, it grounds him. Consider treating him to a Trager massage, where he is gently rocked a thousand times an hour, until his nervous system gives up and blisses out in ecstasy. Always have water nearby . . . a small fountain, a bowl of goldfish, a beautifully appointed bathtub. Let there be music, at all times. He uses it, whether he knows it or not, to soothe and temper his soul. Music can bring him back from the far dark shores when you have all but given up in despair.

## ✳ For His Birthday

The Fish loves luxury and escape, and he loves to go first class. Kidnap him for a night at a four-star hotel or, at the very least, a four-star restaurant. Make sure dinner takes at least three hours. Or try a full-course Japanese banquet, where you are both served endless delectable dishes in an enchanting private room for hours on end.

You could always give him expensive champagne—Pisces adores water and all related fluids. In fact, anything to do with water is a wonderful idea. A small fountain for his porch or a moonlight picnic by the sea or the nearest lake would be wonderful. Or surprise him some night with a softly scented bath, where you appear dressed in not much, hand him a glass of bubbly, and slowly massage his tired muscles with balm of eucalyptus. Balm is what he needs, for the harsh winds of life blow fiercely upon him.